GET TO KNOW
SEVILLE
IN JUST A FEW DAYS

- **EXPLORE THE CITY'S CHARACTER THROUGH ITS CULTURE AND LIFESTYLE.**

- **WIDE SELECTION OF THE BEST ADDRESSES FOR HOTELS, RESTAURANTS, CAFÉS & BARS.**

- **COMPREHENSIVE SHOPPING GUIDE WITH ADDRESSES AND OPENING TIMES.**

- **PLACES OF INTEREST TO VISIT PLUS ADDRESSES AND OPENING TIMES.**

- **350 COLOUR PHO... MAPS.**

- **THE TOP 12 UNMIS... SITES IN DETAIL.**

ISBN 0-5...032

HACHETTE

£4.99 UK
$9.95 US
$14.95 CAN

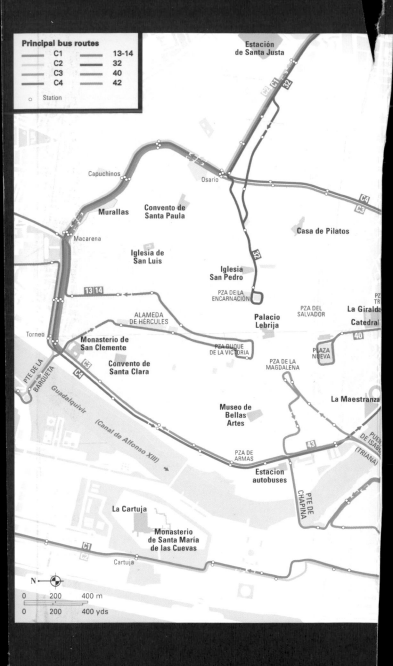

Principal bus routes

—— C1	—— 13-14
—— C2	—— 32
—— C3	—— 40
—— C4	—— 42

o Station

Estación
de Santa Justa

Capuchinos

Osario

Murallas

**Convento de
Santa Paula**

Casa de Pilatos

Macarena

**Iglesia de
San Luis**

**Iglesia
San Pedro**

PZA DE LA
ENCARNACIÓN

13 14

**Palacio
Lebrija**

PZA DEL
SALVADOR

La Giralda

Catedral

ALAMEDA
DE HÉRCULES

40

Torneo

**Monasterio de
San Clemente**

PZA DUQUE
DE LA VICTORIA

PZA DE LA
MAGDALENA

PLAZA
NUEVA

PZA
TR

**Convento de
Santa Clara**

PTE DE LA
BARQUETA

La Maestranza

Guadalquivir

(Canal de Alfonso XIII)

**Museo de
Bellas
Artes**

PUEN
DE (SAB

(TRIANA)

PZA DE
ARMAS

43

**Estación
autobuses**

PTE DE
CHAPINA

La Cartuja

**Monasterio
de Santa María
de las Cuevas**

Cartuja

C1

C2

N

0	200	400 m
0	200	400 yds

USEFUL WORDS AND PHRASES

A basic guide to pronunciation

Spanish is not a difficult language to pronounce, but there are certain things you should know. An accent on a letter shows where the stress of the word should fall. If there is no accent, each syllable is given equal emphasis.

Vowels

Every vowel sound is pronounced and they are generally short:
'a' – 'ah' as in 'park'
'e' – 'eh' as in 'bed'
'o' – 'o' as in 'hot'
'u' – 'ooh' as in 'rule'
'i' – 'ech' as in 'police'

Consonants

With regard to consonants, there are a few sounds which may be new to you:
'c' – before an 'e' it is a 'th' sound in English ('soft c') so 'cebolla' is pronounced 'the-boyah'
'j' is pronounced like an English 'h', so 'jalapeno' becomes 'h-alapeno'
'h' is always silent
'll' – 'y' sound in English, so 'tortilla' is pronounced 'tort-y-ah'
'ñ' is pronounced like the 'ni' in 'onion'
'z' is the same as the 'soft c'

Useful expressions

Yes: *sí*
No: *no*
Please: *por favor*
Thank you very much: *muchas gracias*
You're welcome: *de nada*
Hello: *hola*
Goodbye: *adiós*
Good morning: *buenos días*
Good afternoon: *buenas tardes*
Good night: *buenas noches*
See you tomorrow: *hasta mañana*
Excuse me: *perdóne*
Money: *dinero*
How much is ... ?: *¿cuánto es?*
I don't understand: *no entiendo*
I want: *quiero*
I'd like: *quisiera*
Do you speak English?: *¿habla inglés?*
Madam: *señora*
Sir: *señor*

At customs

Customs: *duana*
Personal items: *objetos personales*
Passport: *pasaporte*
Nothing to declare: *nada a declarar*

At the hotel

Reservation: *reserva*
Room: *habitación*
I would like a room: *quisiera una habitación*
For one night: *para una noche*
For two nights: *para dos noches*
Room with twin beds: *habitación con dos camas separadas*
Single room: *habitación individual*
Double room: *habitación doble*

In the town

Ahead: *adelante*
Bank: *banco*
Bureau de change: *casa de cambio*
On the left: *a la izquierda*
On the right: *a la derecha*
Post office: *oficina de correos*
Public telephone: *cabina*
Street: *calle*
Tourist office: *oficina de turismo*
Traffic light: *semáforo*
Where is?: *¿dónde está?*

At the restaurant

I'd like to reserve a table: *quiero reservar una mesa*
The bill, please: *la cuenta por favor*
Ashtray: *un cenicero*
Beer: *cerveza*
Bottle: *botella*
Bread: *pan*
Breakfast: *desayuno*
Butter: *mantequilla*
Cheese: *queso*
Daily special: *plato del día*
Dessert: *postre*
Dinner: *cena*
Fork: *tenedor*
Knife: *cuchillo*
Lunch: *almuerzo*
Main course: *plato principal*
Meal: *comida*
Meat: *carne*
Menu: *carta*
Pepper: *pimienta*
Plate/dish: *plato*
Salad: *ensalada*
Salt: *sal*
Service included: *servicio incluído*
Spoon: *cuchara*
Starter: *primer plato*
Tip: *propina*
Waiter: *camarero*
Water: *agua*
Wine: *vino*
Wine list: *lista de vinos*

Shopping

How much is it?: *¿Cuánto cuesta?*
In another colour: *de otro color*
It's too expensive: *es demasiado caro*
Do you take credit cards?: *¿acepta tarjetas de credito?*
In cash: *en efectivo*
I'm just looking, thank you: *sólo viendo, gracias*
Antiques: *antigüedades*
Bookshop: *librería*
Department store: *gran almacén*
Jewellers: *joyería*
Market: *mercado*
Newspaper: *periódico*
Pharmacy: *farmacia*
Price: *precio*
Sale: *rebajas*
Shop/Boutique: *tienda*
Size (clothes): *talla*
Size (shoes): *medida*
Supermarket: *supermercado*
Tobacconist: *estanco*

Times and dates

After: *después*
Again: *otra vez*
Before: *antes*
During: *durante*
Early: *temprano*
Hour: *hora*
Late: *tarde*
Minute: *minuto*
Now: *ahora*
Today: *hoy*
Tomorrow: *mañana*
What time is it?: *¿Qué hora es?*
When: *cuándo*
Where: *¿dónde?*
Yesterday: *ayer*

Look on page 134 for more handy words and phrases!

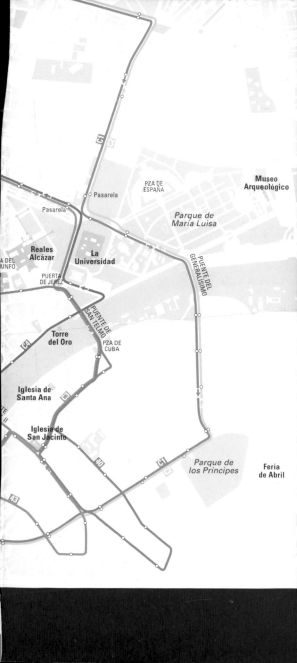

Museo Arqueológico

PZA DE ESPAÑA

Parque de María Luisa

Pasarela

Pasarela

Reales Alcázar

La Universidad

A DEL UNFO

PUERTA DE JEREZ

PUENTE DEL GENERALISIMO

PUENTE DE SAN TELMO

Torre del Oro

PZA DE CUBA

Iglesia de Santa Ana

TE II

Iglesia de San Jacinto

Parque de los Príncipes

Feria de Abril

A GREAT WEEKEND IN
SEVILLE

A GREAT WEEKEND IN SEVILLE

Seville, Hispalis, Isbiliya, this stunning city's name has been continually restyled by the whim of history. A Phoenician trading empire, a leading light in the glory of Rome, host to the fabulous Moorish court or spirit of the age of discovery … Seville's every street corner is an open book to a glorious and magical past that feeds our imaginations. From Santa Cruz, the old Jewish quarter, to the buildings inspired by 16th-century Iberian–American architecture, Seville reflects the melting pot of religions, cultures and distant worlds that forged it.

What is most apparent to visitors is the omnipresence of the Catholic Church – the city is filled with churches, monasteries and convents. Each district, each community reveres its own saint or Virgin. Wherever you go, Sevillians' devotion is palpable and reaches its crescendo during Easter Week. Candle-lit processions of hooded penitents and women in mourning veils pass through the streets which resound with *saetas*, shouts and wails … But Seville is a multi-facetted city and should not be mistaken for a pious bigot shackled by its traditions. The other major event of the year, the April Feria, welcomes spring with an explosion of colours, smells and light. When the sun sets, the Maestranza arena and the Real de la Feria park are lit by thousands of Chinese lanterns heralding the magic of the Andalucian nights to come. For this is the essence of Seville; it comes to life at night. Nobody could claim to know the city unless they have spent at least one evening trawling the bars for tapas and drinks and dancing to the bewitching rhythms of flamenco before finishing up

SHIPPING PURCHASES HOME

If you buy something too bulky to carry home, the antique and interior design shops all have their own shipping agents. They can take care of all the details and your goods will be delivered in about a month. However, take care to find out exactly what fees are involved. To arrange your own carrier try:

UPS
☎ 900 102 410 (freephone)
www.ups.com

Seur Internacional
☎ 902 101 010
www.suerinternacional.com

HOW TO PAY

you prefer to use cash, there e plenty of automatic cash achines (ATMs) available for u to withdraw money using ur Visa or MasterCard. It's t a good idea, however, to ke out more than you really ed as there's a hefty charge r the privilege. Charges are a less if you use your credit rd to pay for goods in stores, d Visa and MasterCard are cepted nearly everywhere – hough it's worth checking ns outside outlets to make re.

In case of lost or stolen cards, contact the relevant centre in Madrid:

American Express
☎ 915 720 303

Visa/MasterCard
☎ 900 974 445

Diners Club
☎ 902 401 112
or 901 101 011

PRICES

Although really good deals are becoming less common in Spain, prices are generally lower than in the UK and there are plenty of bargains to be found. This is particularly true of shoes and leather in general. Certainly wine and some food products are cheaper than at home.

WEEKEND SHOPPING

At weekends, most shops are only open on Saturday mornings. In the afternoon, all but the larger department stores shut up shop. Everything closes on Sunday, which leaves Seville's numerous open-air markets as the only option for dedicated shoppers. The fleamarket at the Alameda de Hércules is one of the best (see p. 100), and there's a

fascinating pet market in the Plaza del Alfalfa, also on a Sunday (see p. 100)

CUSTOMS DUTY

If you're an EU citizen, you won't have to pay any customs duty on your purchases, whatever their value, but you'll need to show the receipts. Non-EU citizens are exempt from paying VAT on purchases over €90 in value. Remember to ask for a 'Tax-free cheque' when making your purchase. On leaving Spain, ensure you have the 'cheques' stamped at customs so that you can cash them at a branch of the Banco Exterior de España when you arrive home. If you buy a work of art or an antique declared as *de valor patrimonial* ('of heritage value'), you'll need an export licence. The vendor can help you with this process and you can insist on a certificate of authenticity. An invoice is essential – you may be asked to produce it at customs and it will be useful if you ever want to sell your purchase at a later date.

VIPS

This nationwide chain has two stores in Seville, one on the Av. República Argentina (23–25, ☎ 954 279 397), and the other in the Nervión Plaza shopping centre (see p. 103). Nominally a drugstore, VIPS also incorporates a bookshop, supermarket and café. Prices are a little higher than elsewhere, but as it's open from 9am to 3am, it's ideal if you need something when everywhere else is closed.

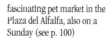

WOMEN'S FASHION

Andalucian women's dress-sense is rather conservative. A group of Spanish designers caters for their preferred classic look with elegant, functional and minimalist styling. Nevertheless, Andalucia has also nurtured a number of talents that have broken free from the rather traditional look. Some, such as Victorio & Lucchino, take their inspiration from Seville's dazzling light and rich folklore in creating their models.

Tony Benítez
C. Placentines, 1 (C3)
☎ 954 563 768
or 954 563 762
Open Mon.-Sat. 10am-2pm, 5.30-8.30pm.

This renowned Sevillian couturier counts the Queen of Spain and her daughters among his clients. He specialises in bridal wear and has also created an off-the-peg range displayed in a showroom overlooking the orange trees on the patio outside his workroom. Known for the careful cut of his cloth and the quality of his materials, Tony Benítez aims to create a look that will remain elegant with the passage of time – in other words, designs for life.

Victorio & Lucchino
C. Sierpes, 87 (C2)
☎ 954 227 951
Open Mon.-Fri. 10.30am-1.30pm, 5.30-8.30pm,
Sat. 10.30am-2pm.

An explosion of colours is the signature of these two Sevillian designers. The unmistakeable proof of their calibre is the esteem in which they are held by Seville's women, the true arbiters of Spanish fashion. Taking their inspiration from Andalucian culture, their collections feature brightly coloured, sheer fabrics, asymmetric frills and filmy silk shawls (*mantones*). You'll also find a collection of *flamenca* dresses, with a contemporary take on traditional style.

Meye Maier
C. Pasaje Vila, 12 (C2)
☎/📠 954 226 575
Open Mon.-Sat. 10am-2pm, 5-8pm.

Stepping into this boutique is like entering a dream world of elegance and softness. It's in this blue-and-white boudoir that the women of Seville select their trousseaus. There's an amazing choice of beautiful peignoirs in quilted cotton, embroidered sheets and superb white tablecloths. Bright colours and natural fibres (cotton, linen, silk) as well as lace, ribbons and fine embroider are the order of the day, creating beautiful clothes in enduring styl

Massimo Dutti

C. Velázquez,
12 (C3)
☎ 954 225 772
Open Mon.-Sat.
10am-9pm.

Part of the popular
Zara group (see p. 84),
this chain tends to be a
little more up-market. The
styles reflect Spanish tastes
and follow the latest trends
with plenty of accessories
on offer, including bags
and some lovely belts,
to complete the look.
Prices aren't as low as
at Zara but they still
represent good value for
money, considering the
quality of the clothes.

Homeless

C. O'Donnell, 16 B (C3)
☎ 954 502 675
www.homeless.es
Open Mon.-Sat.
10am-2pm, 5-
8.30pm.

FASHION, FOLKLORE OR A BIT OF BOTH?

In Andalucia high-fashion and traditional dress go hand-in-hand. The *flamenca* costume is the only regional dress capable of following the latest fashion trends. The patterns, the colours, the fabrics and even the number of frills are variable from one season to the next. What's more, the women of Seville have also retained a number of traditional elements in their day-to-day wear. A good example of this is the *mantoncillo*, a little triangular scarf made from brightly coloured silk or crêpe, which is pure flamenco in origin. It looks fabulous whether slipped over the shoulders of a strapless dress, knotted casually around the neck of a sweater or tied loosely round the waist.

A share of the profits from this shop goes to help the homeless, which explains its name. The inspiration for the designs also comes from street-style and the clothes are youth-oriented with a very casual feel. A level of sophistication is achieved by mixing and matching simple articles with more elaborate items. The overall effect is an original and streetwise look which certainly is not lacking in elegance. There are plenty of accessories to complete the outfits, including simply designed bags in a vast range of colours. Prices are reasonable.

Adolfo Domínguez
C. Sierpes, 2 (C2)
☎ 954 226 538
Open Mon.-Sat., 10am-9pm.

'The classic *is* the avant-garde' claims Adolfo Domínguez, who hails from Galicia in Northern Spain. His designs are typically Spanish in their elegance and classic style. Domínguez is also aiming to make a splash in interior design as well as men and women's fashions, and has developed a range of interior design items, all reflecting his own inimitable style.

Roberto Verino
C. Rioja, 14-16 (C3)
☎ 954 227 151
Open Mon.-Sat. 10am-1.30pm, 5-8.30pm.

This Galician designer has introduced a simple, exciting line of contemporary clothes for men and women. In his up-to-date

boutique, which has become a byword for fashion amongst Seville's youth, you'll find classic tailoring and top quality clothing. A wide range of accessories and perfumes is also available to complete the look.

Loewe
Plaza Nueva,12 (C3)
☎ 954 225 253
Open Mon.-Sat.
10am-2pm,
5-8.30pm.

This classic Spanish brand is already well established in the international world of fashion. It has recently been given a new lease of life thanks to US designer Narciso Rodríguez, who has introduced a slightly more contemporary feel without spoiling the label's characteristic elegance and sophistication. You'll also find an attractive range of bags, luggage and

shoes in the large and glittering boutique, located on Seville's Plaza Nueva.

Zara
C. Rioja, 10 (C3)
☎ 954 211 058
Open Mon.-Sat. 10am-9pm.

Zara has become a household name. This famous Spanish chain has opened branches throughout mainland Europe and the UK and is renowned for being first with the latest trends at remarkable prices. If you get a chance, it's well worth popping in, as the prices are even better here than they are back home.

Antonio Pernas
C. Rosario, 8 (C3)
☎/🖷 954 226 433
Open Mon.-Sat.
10am-2pm,
5.30-9pm.

Every woman's wardrobe should possess a few good pieces based on quality fabrics, natural colours and

REBAJAS!

In Spain, just like everywhere else, the sales (*rebajas*) take place in January and February for the autumn/winter collections and June and July for the spring/summer ranges. The reductions are great, but sadly the sales don't fall during the best time of year for visiting Seville (which is April to May or September to October). Fashion victims face a tough choice.

...ared-down lines. If you're ...oking for well-cut clothes in ...eryday, simple, practical styles ...at never become dated and ...ill stand you in good stead for ... long time, then you've found ...em!

Purificación García

. Rioja, 13 (C3)
☎ 954 563 223
...pen Mon.-Sat. 10am-
...30pm, 5-8.30pm.

...is pretty boutique's very high-
...le interior, laid out over two
...ors, makes use of fresh colours
...d open spaces to give an
...pression of intense brightness.
... you might expect, the clothes
...emselves are similarly bright
...d colourful. Purificación García
...one of the most avant-garde of

the Spanish designer labels. Its high quality collections are always the latest trend and there's also a line of extremely feminine shoes.

Roberto Torretta

C. Rosario, 13 (C3)
☎ 954 228 404
Open Mon.-Sat.
10am-1.30pm,
5.30-9pm.

This designer, who arrived from Argentina in 1972, was one of the revelations of a recent *Pasarela Cibeles* (high-fashion presentation) in Madrid. Unfortunately, his pre-eminence is reflected in his prices. On offer in this tiny boutique, located at the bottom of the Cuesta del Rosario, is an array of classic, elegant designs and beautiful items in leather.

Ropero

Plaza del Pan, 2 (C2)
☎ 954 219 020
Open Mon.-Sat. 10am-2pm,
5-8pm.

This is the sort of place where you might well find a bargain – a second-hand clothes shop with

an eclectic array of fashions from all corners of the world. Everything is in excellent condition and, what's more, shopping here means you're contributing to a worthy cause – recycling. Not a bad idea!

Marisa Martín

C. Argote de Molina, 21 (C2)
☎ 954 219 312
🅕 944 562 521
Open Mon.-Fri.
10am-2pm,
4-8.30pm, Sat.
10am-2pm.

This well-known designer specialises in made-to-measure dresses using sumptuous Italian fabrics. The elegantly-styled results all carry a unique Marisa Martín label and every item is a complete original.

SHOES AND ACCESSORIES

A ndalucian women are fashion-conscious and feminine, and attach a great deal of importance to accessories. As a result, Seville's natural combination of light and colour can be seen in a daily pageant of handbags, jewellery and scarves, all adding brightness to the more conservative fashions. As for shoes, the choice is wide, the quality is excellent and the prices competitive. Shop around and you're bound to find something that you simply can't live without.

browsing for accessories that seem to get more and more alluring. Very dangerous!

Pilar Burgos

C. La Campana, 3 (B3)
☎ 954 226 845
Open Mon.-Sat.
10am-9pm.

This store's great draw is its impressive range of shoes on display which are excellent value for money. It's just the place to find a pair that will exactly match the colour of the dress that you've just bought. Prices start at around €50, which can't be bad.

Africa de Vicente

C. Pedro Pérez Fernández, 25 (D3-E3)
☎ 954 274 184
open Mon.-Sat. 9.30am-1.30pm, 5.30-9pm.

This young Sevillian designer has always believed in showing women at their best without losing sight of practicalities. Few would argue with her opinion that a well-chosen accessory can make all the difference to an outfit. The shoes in her boutique, from the most feminine styles to mules and court shoes, are modern and imaginative but easy to wear. You can spend a happy hour here

Nicolás

C. Sierpes, 49 (C2)
☎ 954 225 878
Open Mon.-Sat. 10am-9pm.

With several outlets in the city, this is one of Seville's best-known shoe stores. The shoes and accessories are all pretty conventional, but very good quality. The prices are attractive and the boutique is beginning to refresh its range of designs and styles, so if you look carefully, you may be able to find items that are a little more daring.

ESPADRILLES GALORE!

With the arrival of summer, a vast selection of espadrilles hits even the most conservative shops. They are comfortable, cheap and fun to wear. The Spanish often go in for the kind that tie high up around the ankle. One word of warning though – don't wear them in the rain. You can buy them at almost any shoe shop in the city centre or Triana, or from a number of specialist stores, especially in Calle San Jacinto (Triana, D4).

arrutx

. Rioja, 13 (C3)
☎ 954 560 019
Open Mon.-Sat.
0am-1.30pm,
.30-9pm.

his established Majorcan
esigner always manages to
splay the smartest feminine
ootwear, which can be matched
with a choice of stylish bags.
he quality is guaranteed and
e prices, for such a famous
ame, are quite affordable.
ur dream shoes will set you
ack between €100 and €150.

Pineda

Plaza Nueva, 12 (C3)
☎ 954 564 249
Open Mon.-Sat. 9.30am-
2pm, 5-8.30pm (closed Sat.
pm in summer).

The owner of this shop, Francisco Javier Rodríguez de Pineda, belongs to a family with a considerable reputation in the world of shoes and leather accessories. He's the brother of the owner of El Caballo (see p. 47), but left the family business ten years ago to set up his own boutique. Since then he has made a name for himself among the most discerning of Seville's clientele. While the men's styles retain a classic sobriety, those for women are substantially more innovative. There's a broad choice and prices vary between €36 and €96 for a pair of shoes and €30 and €150 for a bag, which is excellent considering the quality on offer.

Freesia

C. del Turia, 12 (D3/E3)
☎/♁ 954 273 534
Open Mon.-Sat. 10.30am-
2pm, 5.30-8.30pm.

If you're a bit down in the dumps or the sun's gone in, this place will put a smile back on your face. Freesia is all about colour and offers every imaginable accessory at reasonable prices. The scarves, necklaces and bags make perfect gifts. It's almost impossible to leave empty-handed.

jewellery are simply irresistible. There's something here to please everyone, whatever their taste.

Coco Sevilla

C. Ximénez de Enciso, 2 (C2)
☎ 954 214 532
Open Mon.-Sat. 10am-1.30pm, 5-8.30pm.

If you don't feel you can leave Seville without a souvenir of your stay, you're more than likely to find something to your taste in this shop. Much of its attraction lies in the originality of its wares because it's as much a studio as a shop. The colourful hand-painted patterns on the scarves, *mantones*, fans and silk bags are very appealing.

Nandaiasa

C. Virgen de Fuensanta, 7 (Los Remedios, D3/E3)
☎/📠 954 285 350
Open Mon.-Sat. 10am-2pm, 5-9pm.

The name 'Nandaiasa' is an amalgamation of two names – Nanda and Asa – who are both designers, one from Seville and the other from Sweden. It's an explosive cultural blend, which has produced a showroom packed with a selection of innovative, elegant shoes and accessories. With the help of either Nanda or Asa, you're bound to find something you like. If not, they can still cater for your wildest dreams as they effectively design to order with their own team of talented craftspeople.

Malagata

Plaza del Cristo de Burgos, 9
☎ 954 210 881 (C2)
Open Mon.-Sat. 10am-2pm, 5-8pm.

The range of accessories created for this boutique displays all of Seville's seductive charm. The myriad colours of the scarves and the silver

Cuqui Castellanos

C. Rosario, 8 (C3)
☎ 954 560 996
Open Mon.-Sat. 10am-1.30pm, 5.30-9pm.

At Cuqui Castellanos you'll find the best names and the most sophisticated collections of shoes and accessories from all the big international designers. It's the place to discover the very latest in shoes or that little bag that will make all the difference to your new outfit. Unfortunately the prices are pretty steep (from around €140).

coloured costume jewellery, beautiful antique coral necklaces and little silver handbags.

Nuria Cobo

C. Mendez Nuñez, 14 (C3)
☎/🖷 954 210 603
C. O'Donnell, 26 (C3)
☎/🖷 954 217 088
Open Mon.-Sat. 10am-1.30pm, 5-8.30pm.

As well as beautiful shoes in classic styles, this shop has a selection of sandals and espadrilles that have been revamped in a contemporary, original style. They are pretty funky, some would say over-the-top, and full of the brightness and joy of the city.

Elena Bernal

C. Sierpes, 59 (C2)
☎ 954 226 138
Open Mon.-Sat. 10am-1.30pm, 5.30-9pm.

Elena Bernal first started with a shop selling accessories for *flamenca* costumes. It was such a success that once she had established herself in the hearts and minds of Seville's fashion-conscious public, she was able to open several more clothing and accessory shops. You'll see her name quite frequently along Calle Sierpes and at no. 59 she has an accessory shop. There's a wide choice to suit all budgets, including, amongst other things in her large collection, brightly

Cuero's Calle

C. Cardenal Spinola, 5 (B3)
Open Mon. Fri. 10am-2pm, 5-9pm, Sat. 10.30am-2pm.

DUBLOS, A PAIR OF AVANT-GARDE DESIGNERS

C. San Vicente, 67 (B3)
☎/🖷 954 386 129
Open Mon.-Sat. 9.30am-1.30pm, 4.30-8.30pm.

When it comes to accessories, Andalucian designers Alonso and Pepe love to explore every possible creative avenue. Their work has appeared on stage in shows such as *The Barber of Seville*, embellishing costumes designed by Victorio & Lucchino. It's quite astonishing to see what can be achieved with crystal, coral, bronze, semi-precious stones, cord and shells. You can visit their workshop, but it's best to call beforehand. They can also tell you which shops stock their range of products.

Located near the Plaza de la Gavina, this place is a real kingdom of leather. It specialises in selling and repairing leather garments, bags, briefcases, luggage and gloves. They even stock a selection of leather swimsuits – waterproofed, naturally.

MEN'S FASHION

Spanish men, and Andalucians in particular, are the epitome of classic elegance. They love tradition, the countryside, horsemanship and hunting, and eschew the dash and originality of their womenfolk. They can be demanding and pleasure loving, with a strong appreciation of quality. The clothes on offer to the gentlemen of Seville tend to be well cut, in natural fabrics and subdued colours – making them a tempting proposition whatever your nationality.

Jara y Sedal
C. Adriano, 16 (C3)
☎ 954 222 319
or 954 214 250
Open Mon.-Sat. 10am-2pm, 5-8pm.

Lovers of the great outdoors will find every garment and accessory they could possibly need for a hunting or fishing trip in this specialist shop. It also offers a selection of smaller items, which are perfect for gifts, from umbrellas to ceramics painted with hunting motifs.

Deportes 'Z'
C. Sierpes, 41 (C2)
☎ 954 500 272
C. Imagén, 7 (C2)
☎ 954 500 244
Open Mon.-Sat. 10am-2pm, 5-8pm.

'Z' stands for Zulategui, the name of the family that has owned this concern since it first opened. It started life as a gunsmith and opposite the Calle Sierpes store you can see the word 'Armería' written on the tiled wall, which is now a listed historical feature. With several stores in Seville, Deportes 'Z' is the biggest chain of sports shops in the city.

Heracles
C. Villegas, 1 (C2)
☎ 954 502 022
🕿 954 502 256
Open Mon.-Sat.
10am-2pm, 5-8pm.

Seeking out presents for men is a notoriously difficult task, but this shop offers a wide selection of original and practical ideas. The huge choice will fire your imagination and help you find the ideal gift. There are all sorts of different stationery items, colourful umbrellas, silk ties, trendy braces and even an alarm clock that will wake the man in your life up gently!

Camper
C. Tetuán, 24 (C3)
☎ 954 222 811
Open Mon.-Fri. 10am-2pm, 4.30-8.30pm, Sat. 10am-8.30pm.

Camper is a Spanish chain that has enjoyed great success with its fresh style and imaginative products. With shops opening all across Europe and even in Australia, Japan and other parts of the world, its range of sports and leisure footwear has become highly popular. In this central boutique you'll find the very latest creations, as well as many affordable popular classic lines.

MAQUEDANO

C. Sierpes, 40 (C2)
☎ 954 564 771
Open Mon.-Sat.
10am-2pm, 5-8pm.

This shop, founded in 1896, is the ideal place to find a traditional *sombrero cordobés* (Cordoban hat). As it's well known for offering the last word in Spanish headgear, the shop is well frequented by a showbiz clientele. If you're not sure, feel free to ask the owner for advice on

how the various models of hats should be worn – there's a whole series of customs to be followed if you don't want to stand out as a tourist.

Lester

C. Muñoz Oliv (C3)
☎ 954 222 820
✆ 954 22 32 05
**Open Mon.-Sat. 10am-2pm,
5-8pm.**

When it first opened, Lester specialised in classic silk ties in a number of colourful designs. On the back of that initial success, it has now widened its stock to include other male fashion accessories as well as a range of silk scarves for women. The excellent quality ties boast original designs and are currently offered at very affordable prices.

Arcab

**Paseo de Cristobal
Colón, 18 (C3)**
☎ 954 561 421
or 954 218 130
www.arcab.es
**Open Mon.-Fri. 9.30am-
1.30pm, 5-8.30pm,
Sat. 10am-2pm.**

This shop is a paradise for people who love equestrian pursuits. With more than 20 years' experience, the quality of Arcab's range is second to none. It offers a range of clothing and equipment for riders and for their horses, including brushes and horse care products, as well as a selection of giftware. The very comprehensive website is well worth a browse.

Pull & Bear

C. O'Donell, 9 (C3)
☎ 954 561 128
www.pullbear.com
**Open Mon.-Sat.
10am-9pm.**

The clothes here are aimed at a younger clientele, with a style markedly different to the collections found in the majority of Seville's boutiques. Its large, slightly futuristic showroom reflects the more modern, sportswear-

inspired designs of today. For those waiting for their companions to finish shopping, there's even a reading area where you can browse through a selection of art books, which are also for sale.

FOR CHILDREN

They are better at spoiling their children in Andalucia than anywhere else in Spain. Whether it's haute couture or outlets specialising in more traditional wear, nothing is too good for their little angels, who are welcomed into the shops as if they were established customers, with

no effort spared to cater to their whims. As a result, Seville has an astonishing number of stores dedicated to children, and they strive hard to appeal to their young clients – as well as their parents.

B&B Niños

C. Rosario, 17 (C3)
☎ 954 275 122
Open Mon.-Sat. 10am-2pm, 5-8pm.

Parents find it all too easy to relive their own childhoods when it comes to creating the ideal space for their children. However, a child's bedroom, which has to fill so many functions, from playroom to hideaway, can be difficult to design. B&B Niños can provide all the furniture for a child's room made to measure, including wardrobes, beds, nappy-changing units, cots – they simply think of everything. The shop has a splendid play area filled with toys, and also stocks a range of clothing for 0 to 16-year-olds by all the well-known brands. Another branch (B&B Premama) at no.12 in the same street specialises in maternity wear and products.

Entre Arte

Las Casitas de Adela
C. Paseo Colón, 18 (C3)
☎ 954 216 111
Open Mon.-Sat. 10am-2pm, 5-8pm.

Entre Arte is a very unusual and curious shop that's as much fun for adults as it is for children. It's a fantasy world dedicated to

dolls' houses, all of which are handmade by local craftsmen. Every imaginable item is made to scale, and the detail on each tiny object is out of this world. The shop is run by Josela Fernández, who also specialises in restoring dolls' houses in his small workshop at the back of the shop.

José Jaén Morillo Merceria Anan Mary

C. Castilla, 60 (C4)
☎ 954 332 789
Open Mon.-Fri. 9.30am-
1.30pm, 5.30-8.30pm.,
Sat. 9.30am-1.30pm.

This haberdasher's isn't much to look at and you probably wouldn't think twice about going in unless someone suggested it. But if you bypass the ladies' lingerie and head straight for the children's clothing department, you'll find adorable little cotton and embroidered outfits (0–8 years) which are not only well-made but also reasonably priced.

Imaginarium

Asunción, 38 (E3-D3)
☎ 954 284 345
C. Rivero, 10 (C3)
☎ 954 584 657
www.imaginarium.es
Open Mon.-Sat. 10am-
2pm, 5-8pm.

If your little ones have had enough of shops for grown-ups then Imaginarium is the place to take them. It's a Mecca of fun for young visitors looking for adventure and discovery. Games, books, toys – this emporium of play and creativity has the lot. Energetic staff are on hand to demonstrate the latest crazes and to answer all the questions. In this fairyland everyone can play to their heart's content and tears and tantrums are definitely not allowed.

Catedral Pibe

Av. Constitución, 20
(C2-3)
☎ 954 221 900
Open Mon.-Sat.
10am-2pm, 5-8pm.

With four shops and years of experience, Catedral Pibe has earned the trust of the parents of Seville.

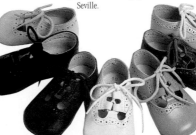

They stock beautifully elegant little shoes that are perfect for weddings or other big occasions, including court shoes for the girls and moccasins for the boys. For less formal, everyday wear, there are cute little ballet shoes and lace-up boots that really support developing bones. The shop also carries a wide range of socks.

Blanca Hogar

C. Asunción, 6 (D3-E3)
☎ 954 277 741
Open Mon.-Sat. 10am-2pm,
5-8pm.

Blanca Hogar specialises in children's bed linen with a choice of brightly coloured sheets for little beds, decorated with flowers or tartan, and pillow cases in soft fabrics and warm

colours. The shop is very pleasantly decorated with simple white walls and exposed brickwork and also stocks attractive fabrics, wallpaper and towels.

INTERIOR DESIGN

Forget plastic and Formica. In Seville you can rethink and restyle your home with colourful *azulejos*, beautiful ceramics and traditional sculpture. That's not to say that the city will dampen any enthusiasm for modern objects, or the clean lines of contemporary minimalist designs. And if you prefer natural finishes, then you can find an abundance of objects made from wood, raffia, rattan and other natural materials as well as exotic furniture from faraway places.

Trazos
C. O'Donnell, 13 (C3)
☎ 954 225 825
Open Mon.-Sat. 10am-2pm, 5-8pm.

Trazos sells a range of very stylish contemporary furniture for offices and dining rooms. The exclusively Spanish designs are well worth a look.

Alquitara
C. de Francos, 44 (C2)
☎ 954 215 234
Open Mon.-Sat. 10am-2pm, 5-8pm.

Taller Cuatro
C. Rosario, 4 (C3)
☎ 954 210 208
℻ 954 561 186
Open Mon.-Sat. 10am-2pm, 5-8pm

You won't be disappointed if you're tempted inside by this shop's beautifully arranged window display. The interior is decorated all in white apart from the brightly coloured objects – African and Indonesian furniture, as well as more simple, functional pieces – displayed to good effect in the minimalist design. It's also a good place to find unusual little gifts to take home.

This beautiful store is arranged over two floors displaying classic, elegant designs whose pure lines echo the essence of modern interior decoration. Alquitara isn't just a temple to modernity, however; timeless Andalucian-style china and traditional ceramics are also available, making it a good place to put together a wedding list.

Santa Teresa
C. Muñoz y Pabón, 1 (C2)
☎ 954 216 353
Open Mon.-Sat. 10am-2pm,
5-8pm.

This store, which could easily be mistaken for a church or museum, is actually an art and interior design shop. It's difficult to know where to start in this extraordinary place, which is full of religious sculpture and paintings by 19th and 20th-century artists such as Roberto Domingo, García Ramo and Sánchez Ferrer. It's a delight to browse in this holy of holies for anyone who loves beautiful things.

ceramics. The store itself is decorated in modern style with white walls, and mounts regular exhibitions of Andalucian ceramics, fabrics and hand-woven carpets.

La Indiana
C. Cuna, 17 (C2)
☎ 954 223 783
Open Mon.-Sat. 10am-2pm,
5-8pm.

At La Indiana, fabrics, drapes and decorative items take pride of place, but wood carvings by craftsmen from all four corners of the globe also add an exotic touch. Apart from the Indonesian antiques and the carved wooden sofas, keep an eye out for the Moroccan tea services and West African bowls. The fabrics and Indian bedspreads are also superb.

Ferreteria y fundiciones
C. Luis Montoto, 142A (C1)
☎ 954 573 906
Open Mon.-Fri. 9am-1.30pm, 5-8.30pm,
Sat. 10am-2pm.

Welcome to the world of wrought iron. Located in the city's newest and most up-to-date commercial district, this huge shop is definitely the biggest of its kind in Seville. It's packed with anything and everything you can think of – lamps, picture frames, mirrors, bird cages, coffee tables and designer chairs – all manufactured from wrought iron.

BESUR
C. Aguilas, 21 (B2)
☎ 954 218 135
beacula@mixmail.com
Open Mon.-Sat. 10am-1.30pm, 5.30-8.30pm.

Located right next to the Casa de Pilatos, this traditional craft shop should not be missed. It's stuffed with *azulejos* and ceramics to suit all tastes, as well as a superb collection of top-quality glassware. Remember, delivery can easily be arranged to pretty much anywhere in the world.

Iconos
Av.de la Constitución, 21A (C2-3)
☎ 954 221 408
Open Mon.-Sat. 10am-2pm, 5-8pm.

This is a souvenir shop with a difference. Rather than just the usual tawdry selection of touristy knick-knacks, Iconos stocks traditional and avant-garde ceramics, fans in every style and hand-painted silk fabrics which are revealed in their true light as real works of contemporary art. This is anything but run-of-the-mill and on no account should it be missed.

Munda Interior
. Bailen, 22 (C3)
☎ 954 565 066
Open Mon.-Sat. 10am-2pm, -8pm.

In this furniture and interior accessories shop you can also find out how to use traditional techniques to create avant-garde

CERAMICS, *AZULEJOS* AND POTTERY

Seville's ceramics, whether from Triana or La Cartuja, or in Moorish, Andalucian or 'designer' style, are never anything less than astonishing. You'll come across plenty of opportunities to watch the craftsmen at work and though the skills they use may be centuries old, the results would grace the most contemporary of interiors. The traditional potter's art has been adapted to modern decorative demand, so we can still enjoy its exquisite beauty today.

Sevillarte
C. Sierpes, 66 (C3)
☎ 954 212 836
Open Mon.-Sat. 10am-1.30pm, 2.30-8.15pm.

This renowned shop offers a selection of two distinct styles: modern, colourful ceramics in a contemporary 'Mondrian' style and ceramics inspired by traditional Mudéjar art, which are highly stylised and covered in floral motifs, typical of Moorish design. The blue and white

earthenware dishes and plates are more decorative than practical and would liven up any kitchen wall. Watch the prices, though, they're a little steep.

Cerámica Santa Ana
C. San Jorge, 31 (C3)
☎/🖷 954 333 990
Open Mon.-Fri. 9.30am-1.30pm, 5-8.30pm,
Sat. 10am-2pm.

A thousand and one objects are displayed in this shop, which is stacked with vases, earthenware jars, figurines of the Virgin and

POTTERY AND CERAMICS IN TRIANA

Traditional tile-making techniques are alive and well in Triana. The area is filled with fine boutiques where you can still find 'Triana blue' pottery and ceramics. Take a stroll down streets such as Calle García de Vinuesa, Calle San Jorge, or the tiny cobbled Calle Antillano Campos and you'll see plenty of examples of this famously distinctive colour. You can visit working pottery studios at nos. 20 and 22 Calle Alfarería (C4).

...ints, tiles and even ...eramic chess pieces. ...his huge store is ...evoted to the ...urest traditions ...f Triana's ...eramic ...story ...d has ...tablished ...self as one of ...e best-stocked ...d best-known ...ops in the area. ...hind its beautiful ...e-work frontage you'll ...d a treasure trove of top ...ality art ceramics as well as ...assic and traditional pottery, all ...reasonable prices.

...erámica Santa ...sabel

...Antillano Campos, 9 (C3-4)
... 954 333 945
...pen Mon.-Sat. 10am-2pm,
...8pm.

...is huge shop is the outlet for ...e Santa Isabel factory and was ...ablished in 1789. It looks more ...e a warehouse or a supermarket

...n a shop selling traditional ...ery and the rows of shelves ...play a huge range of every ...d of ceramic – earthenware ..., flower-pots, coloured bowls, ...es, lamps, earthenware floor ...s for kitchens and bathrooms ... antique *azulejos*. You'll find ...embarrassment of riches and ...ndless choice.

La Alacena

C. Alfonso XII, 25 (B3-C3)
☎ 954 228 021
lacartuja@arrais.es
Open Mon.-Sat. 10am-2pm,
5-8pm.

La Alacena caters for the more discerning customer who demands high quality and sophistication. This top-of-the-range display of traditional regional artistry includes the special 'Ciento Cincuenta Aniversario' (150-year anniversary) series, which celebrates La Cartuja's famous ceramic heritage and has been in production for 150 years.

Cerámica Terra

C. Antillano Campos, 3 (C3-4)
☎ 954 340 908
Open Mon.-Fri. 10.30am-
noon, 5-8.30pm,
Sat. 10am-2pm.
The factory is located at
C. Alfareria, 45
☎ 954 344 370

Despite being located in one of Triana's most traditional streets, Cerámica Terra has developed a new form of ceramic expression which, although it follows the traditional techniques, constitutes a virtual revolution in the pottery world. But the golden rule remains: quality and aestheticism take precedence over quantity. The designs are exquisite and every item is made by hand, which makes every piece unique and highly sought after.

EL TORNO

Plaza del Cabildo (C3)
☎ 954 219 190
Open Mon.-Sat.
10am-2pm, 5-8pm.

El Torno only stocks products that have been made in the city's convents, such as traditional sweets, furniture, clothing, rosewood rosaries, linens, trays and baskets. It makes a change from ceramics.

ANTIQUES AND CURIOS

Antique lovers will have no trouble finding specialist shops in the city centre, notably around the Plaza del Alfalfa and towards Calle Cabeza del Rey Don Pedro. There are more than enough antique shops in Seville to satisfy bargain hunters as well as collectors on the lookout for an original or rare piece from the region's rich heritage – just the job for a special gift.

El Mercadillo de Teresa

C. Jeronimo Hernandez, 6-8 or C. Velarde, 3 (B2)
☎ 954 229 810
Open Mon.-Fri. 11am-2pm, 5-8pm, Sat. 11am-2pm.

This shop is an Aladdin's cave of antiquities of every kind, including furniture and curios from Andalucia's past. It's a wonderful chance to find vintage shawls, antique ceramics and wrought iron oddments. Everything is very reasonably priced and when it comes to unearthing the perfect present, you'll be spoilt for choice.

Angel Luis Friazza Rodriguez Anticuario

C. Zaragoza, 48 (C3)
☎ 954 223 567
Open Mon.-Fri. 11am-2pm, 5-9.30pm, Sat. 11am-2pm.

Located in a traditional house with its superb tiled decor, this shop's emphasis is very much on cosmopolitan diversity. The owner may not be the most welcoming person in the world, but she may tempt you with some fine antique artefacts such as paintings and furniture in a number of European styles (as well as a few Asian examples), baroque figures of Christ on the Cross, china and silver services and even bronze busts or Indian furniture. It's decidedly eclectic.

Arquimesa

C. Fernández y González, 15 (C3)
☎ 954 224 540
𝔽 954 212 743
Open Mon.-Fri. 11.30am-2pm, 5.30-8.30pm, Sat. 11.30-2pm.

This very reputable antique dealership has carved out a niche for itself in supplying British and French antique furniture – fairly classical pieces but with an abiding quality. There are also interesting items from further afield and some fine rustic furniture, perfect for a country retreat.

El Niño Seise

Plaza de la Pescadería, 4 (C2)
☎ 954 561 916
**Open Mon.-Sat. 11am-2pm,
4-8pm.**

El Niño Seise is best known for traditional Andalucian antiques and furniture. But don't be too surprised if you also happen upon English wardrobes and tables hidden amongst all the regional bric-à-brac. As far as the latter is concerned, with luck you might come across hand-embroidered silk scarves, tortoiseshell combs, delicate lace veils or toiletry items carved in ivory and coral.

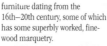

furniture dating from the 16th–20th century, some of which has some superbly worked, fine-wood marquetry.

Antigüedades Morales Ortega

C. Jamerdana, 2 (C2)
**☎ 954 223 606
or 600 218 851**
**Open Mon.-Fri.
11.30am-2.30pm, 5-8pm,
Sat. 11.30am-2.30pm.**

If you happen to be in the old Jewish quarter, try to find time to drop into this little shop The dinner services and old engravings of Seville through the centuries are particularly recommended.

La Judería

Plaza Alfalfa, 5 (C2)
☎ 954 563 833
**Open Mon.-Sat. 11am-2pm,
4-8pm.**

This large antique shop deals mainly in religious paintings, of which there's a huge assortment. You'll also find a collection of

Antigüedades Lola Ortega

**Plaza del Cabildo
(opposite the cathedral, C3)**
☎/📠 954 218 771.

You should know that in this shop you're dealing with one of the city's top specialists in paintings, sculpture and gilding. The Ortega

FÉLIX COLECCIONISMO Y ANTIGÜEDADES

**Av. de la Constitución, 26
(C2–3)**
☎/📠 954 218 026
www.poster-felix.com
Open Mon.-Sat. 11am-2pm and 5-8pm.

Situated next to the post office, this rather narrow and unusual shop specialises in traditional maps and posters. There's a wide variety of them pinned up on the walls – advertising posters, bullfight posters and spring festival posters very like the ones on display in the Museo de Artes y Costumbres Populares (see p. 50), as well as photos of Seville's best-known landmarks. In other words, a treasure trove for both collectors and amateur enthusiasts alike who are hunting for that elusive gem which will make their day worthwhile.

family are passionate advocates of Sevillian antiques and offer a fine collection of jewellery, fans, Chinese porcelain, old clocks, relics and souvenirs from a bygone age.

R.T.

C. Montecarmelo, 20 (D3-E3)
☎ 954 271 130
**Open Mon.-Fri. 11am-2pm,
5-8pm, Sat. 11am-2pm.**

This dealer is a big specialist in European furniture, all made in a vast array of handsomely coloured woods. They also stock old sewing-boxes that have been converted into games tables in this very tastefully presented shop, run by a pair of locals who are both enthusiastic and very welcoming, which never hurts.

MARKETS AND FLEAMARKETS

With such an abundance of green open spaces in the city, it's little wonder that so many traditional markets have sprung up. For the locals they provide yet another excuse for taking a stroll in the open-air. All over the city these markets vie with each other as to which has the best local crafts or specialist foods, but whichever one you patronise, you're sure to get a good taste of authentic Sevillian atmosphere.

Rastro del Parque Alcosa
Sun. morning (off map).

Another fleamarket, also known as the gypsy market, held every Sunday morning in the Parque Alcosa, which is located north-east of the city centre. Each vendor will be happy to spend time telling you about the goods on his stall. In amongst the old bric-à-brac, you'll find people selling clothing, shoes and accessories, as well as lamps and furniture, all at bargain prices.

Alameda de Hércules
Thurs. and Sun. 8am-1pm (B2–3).

Held in the Barrio de la Macarena every Thursday and Sunday morning, this is Seville's oldest and biggest traditional market. Fringed with cafés and tapas bars, but far removed from the tourist hordes, the Alameda de Hércules fleamarket is proving ever more popular. On public holidays, all kinds of old bric-a-brac is piled up on rugs, stalls and even on the ground. Whether you're in search of antiques, flamenco costumes or tools and utensils, both old and new, you'll find them here.

La Plaza de Cabildo
Sun. morning (C3).

This specialist market for stamp and coin collectors takes place every Sunday morning in a pretty little square at the end of the Avenida de la Constitución. You can swap and sell here as well as buy, and the relaxed atmosphere is a real pleasure for philatelists, who can sometimes make astonishing finds.

The Alfalfa pet market
Plaza del Alfalfa (C2). Sun. morning.

This pet market is open to the public as well as professional dealers. It takes place in the

A HISTORIC ESPLANADE

The celebrated Alameda de Hércules – named after the city's founder – is built on former marshland that was drained in 1574. It was thanks to the enterprise of the Count of Barajas that it was turned into this tree-lined boulevard, considered one of the most elegant in Europe during Spain's Golden Age, with its twin Roman statues of Julius Caesar and Hercules. By the 19th century, however, it had deteriorated into a dusty meeting place for the less salubrious members of society and today, it's the haunt of prostitutes at night.

...aza del Alfalfa, where the hay ...r was once held. This small ...e-lined square, surrounded by ...fés, is taken over by hundreds ...different animals every Sunday ...orning, which makes for a ...ally wonderful, if a little

raucous, atmosphere. Some people come here looking to buy a pet cat, while others come to sell their own *cachoros* – baby animals. Every conceivable accessory for your pet is also available, from flea collars, and birdseed to winter coats for dogs.

Craft market
Plaza Duque de la Victoria (B3-C3)
Open Thurs.-Sat. 10am-9pm.

Just to the south of the Barrio de la Macarena, this little craft market takes place three times a week, on Thursdays, Fridays and Saturdays, between 10am and 9pm on the Plaza de la Victoria and the Plaza de la Magdalena. The atmosphere is fairly hippy, reflecting the cosmopolitan nature of the goods on sale. You can find stalls selling anything from costume jewellery to solid silver pieces, scarves, T-shirts and Peruvian wool products.

Marché de Triana
Calle Alfalfa (C2)
Open Mon.-Sat. 7am-4pm.

This covered food market (entrance on the Calle Alfalfa), located in an area better known for its ceramic workshops, opens

between 7am and 4pm, Monday to Saturday. A wide variety of local produce is available, such as hams, olives, olive oil, cheeses and dried flowers. Tourists are scarce and you can enjoy the wonderful local atmosphere. Amongst the other food markets, the Ortiga market deals almost exclusively with organic produce and is held on Tuesdays between 6 and 9pm and on Wednesdays, Thursdays and Fridays between 11am and 2pm and 6 and 9pm. It takes place in the San Lorenzo district, at no. 4 Calle Cristo del Buen Fin. Excellent quality produce can also be found at the markets in Plaza de la Encarnación and El Arenal.

DEPARTMENT STORES AND SHOPPING CENTRES

It's well worth giving the big Spanish stores a try – such as El Corte Inglés ('the English Style'), a highly successful chain popular with Seville's shoppers. Some reasonably sized shopping centres have recently opened their doors, offering a selection of different shops and boutiques. These are always a pleasant place to shop and make it easy to find that vital last minute present.

local crafts, bookshops, food halls, gadgets and souvenir shops. You should be able to find any extra presents you need without too much difficulty. In fashion, all the famous international and Spanish labels are represented, with Zara at the top of the list. Their Home department also offers a wide range of furniture, lighting and other accessories for home interiors. If you're a little fussy in your eating habits and you've had your fill of *jamón Serrano*, you'll be pleased to hear that the cafeteria does a range of delicious little Scandinavian-style open sandwiches.

El Corte Inglés
Plaza del Duque de la Victoria, 7 and 13 (B3-C3)
☎ 954 220 931
Plaza de la Magdalena, 1 (C3)
☎ 954 217 777
C. San Pablo, 1 (C3)
☎ 954 218 855
Open every day 10am-8pm.

You can get pretty much anything you need for day-to-day living in this huge department store. More than 500,000 items are stocked in over 200 departments, including franchises for well-known international brands,

Plaza de Armas
Plaza de la Legión (C3)
Marques de Paradas
☎ 954 908 282
📠 954 903 998
Open every day until 2am.
Shops open Mon.-Sat. 10am-10pm.

This brand-new shopping and leisure complex looks more like a Mudéjar-style palace than a shopping mall. Its remarkably ostentatious appearance is, frankly, somewhat pretentious. Arranged over two floors and with a huge courtyard for added

EL CORTE INGLÉS,
A RETAIL SUCCESS STORY

The story begins in 1890, when a little tailor's shop opened up in Madrid under the name 'El Corte Inglés'. Nearly 40 years later, in 1935, the business was bought by Don Ramón Areces, originally from Asturias in Northern Spain, who transformed it into a clothing store after the Civil War. By the beginning of the 1970s, the company had opened up branches abroad and was by far the biggest chain of department stores in Spain. There are six branches in Seville alone, mostly concentrated around the pedestrianised shopping areas and each with its particular speciality. El Corte Inglés is also famous for the wide range of services it offers, including interpreters, currency exchange, restaurants, cafés, hairdressers and travel agents. You can get just about anything you want here.

area before dispersing into the centre's fast-food outlets, tapas bars and restaurants.

San Pablo
Plaza de Armas Shopping Complex
C. Murillo, 11 (C3)
☎ **954 908 823**
Open Mon.-Sat. 10am-10pm.

If you're in the Plaza de Armas, it's worth dropping in on this little boutique dedicated to horses and riding. The atmosphere is distinctly equestrian and the quality excellent, as you'd expect from something so quintessentially Sevillian.

...harm, the Plaza de Armas contains a huge number of boutiques offering an infinite range of products. Innovative developments include a children's play area and some open-air restaurants.

Nervión Plaza
v. Luis de Morales (off map)
☎ **954 987 082**
Shops open Mon.-Sat. 10am-10pm.

...nother brand-new shopping centre has recently been opened in Seville's most modern quarter, on the corner of Avenida Eduardo Dato and Avenida Luis de Morales, not far from one of the ubiquitous Corte Inglés stores. Nervion Plaza plays host to a variety of shops – bookstores, a supermarket, clothes and accessory boutiques, beauty parlours and even several cinema screens. Built on a number of levels and arranged in a large circle, the centre is also the entrance to the Sanchez Pizjuan football stadium and on match days the place is heaving. After the game, supporters meet in the open-air entrance

GASTRONOMIC DELIGHTS

Tapas bars and restaurants are not the only places where you can enjoy the pleasure of sampling local specialities and produce. You can buy goodies from some of the bars as well as from specialist shops, where the food often comes vacuum-packed or preserved in tins, making it easy to transport. Make the most of this opportunity to take some of Seville's culinary delicacies home in your suitcase.

Tierra Nuestra

C. Constancia, 41 (D4)
☎ 954 552 119
Open Mon.-Fri. 10am-2pm, 5-9pm, Sat. 10am-2pm.

If you've tasted a Spanish wine you enjoyed and want to buy a few bottles to take home, Tierra Nuestra is just the place to come. It offers the best selection of fine Spanish wines in town. The atmosphere is civilized, the staff are highly professional, and satisfaction is virtually guaranteed.

Molino Pintado

C. Arfe, 11 (C3)
C. Betis, 20 (C3)
☎ 954 563 053
or 954 001 055
Open every day noon-1am.

There are two branches of El Molino in Seville. The picturesque little bar located on Calle Arfe offers a wide selection of local produce and the much larger bar, on Calle Betis, has tables where you can sample tapas as well as

a well-stocked shop, selling a variety of delicacies such as charcuterie from Huelva, Ronda cheeses, Xérès vinegar, local preserves and, of course, olive oil.

denominación de origen (labels of authenticity), and a superb collection of Spanish wines.

Supermercados Baco

Plaza Ponce de León, 15 (B/C2)
☎ 954 212 827
Open Mon.-Fri. 9.30am-2.30pm, 5.30-9.30pm, Sat. 9.30am-2.30pm.

Fine foods at wholesale prices! This store has five branches in Seville and specialises in cod (*bacalao*). They also stock *jamón de bellota*, the best cheeses, all with

Everything is well-priced and packaged with the traveller in mind so that it's easy to carry back home.

BAR TIENDA

The best way to decide which local food to take home with you is to taste it first. At any of the *bar tiendas* (bar boutiques), which you'll find scattered around the city, you can order a glass of wine with a portion of tapas and then purchase some of the dish you've just sampled. The Mesón de la Infanta, for one, is highly recommended (see p. 77).

Taberna del Alabardero

C. Zaragoza, 20 (C3)
☎ 954 502 721
📠 954 563 666
Open Mon.-Fri. 10am-9pm,
Sat.-Sun. 11.30am-9.30pm.

This fine restaurant (see p. 72), home to Seville's famous Hotel School, has recently opened a small delicatessen. The little shop, which

the high quality of its produce. It's also very popular with those visitors who appreciate the local gastronomy. If you want a real feast when you get back home, pick up some charcuterie from the Sierra de Huelva, some olive oil and, for a genuine paella, some saffron for a lot less than

you would pay back home. They also offer a selection of organic produce.

prices are slightly steeper than elsewhere but the quality is unquestionably excellent. If you're not convinced, you can always ask to taste a little and you'll soon be swayed.

Convento de San Leandro

Plaza de San Leandro (C2)
Open Mon.-Fri. 9am-1pm,
4-7pm.

It's rather ironic that it should be nuns who tempt us into the sin of gluttony, but as the saying goes, the proof is in the pudding, or more specifically in the *yemas de San Leandro*. These delicious little cakes are available in the city's supermarkets but you can kill two birds with one stone by visiting the convent itself where they are fresher and cheaper. Remember, if a nun greets you with the words '*Ave María Purísima*' ('Hail Mary most pure'), the correct response is '*Sin pecado concebida*' ('conceived without sin').

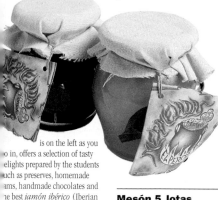

is on the left as you go in, offers a selection of tasty delights prepared by the students such as preserves, homemade jams, handmade chocolates and the best *jamón ibérico* (Iberian ham). You can buy with confidence.

Almacén del Reloj

C. Arfe, 18 (C3)
☎ 954 222 460
Open Mon.-Sat. 9am-9pm.

This little family-run business is popular with the locals as much for its excellent service as

Mesón 5 Jotas

C. Castelar, 1 (C2)
☎ 954 215 863
Open Mon.-Fri. 9am-8pm, Sat. 10am-2pm.

If you want to buy some Iberian ham and be sure of getting the best, you can depend on this specialist supplier. The

FESTIVAL REGALIA

Seville's religious and folkloric traditions are particularly rich. Whenever the opportunity arises, which is fairly often as there's any number of popular festivals to celebrate, the traditional costumes and accessories are pressed into service. Every costume is planned down to the smallest detail and each outfit becomes part of any festive occasion's display of light, colours and music as you will doubtless see – the locals rarely need an excuse to start dancing and singing.

THE *FLAMENCA* DRESS OF SEVILLIAN WOMEN

Lina

C. Lineros, 17 (C2)
☎ 954 212 423
Open Mon.-Fri. 10am-2pm, 5.30-8.30pm, Sat. 10am-2pm.

Lina is the quintessential *flamenca* dress supplier. They make costumes for many famous Spanish flamenco artists and the shop has also been responsible for the costumes for several films. Even the Queen of Spain is a client. You should be aware that these dresses are exclusively made to measure.

Modas Muñoz

C. Cerrajería, 5 (C2-3)
☎ 954 228 596
Open Mon.-Fri. 10am-2pm, 5-8pm, Sat. 10am-2pm

This is the perfect shop to buy your dream *flamenca* dress off the peg. Whether you're after a particular cut, fabric or colour, there's such a choice you're bound to find the right dress and the accessories to go with it. The huge selection allows you to play with a variety of combinations until you've found something original that suits you. They also supply the man's outfit, the *traje de corto*, based on traditional riding apparel, with its short jacket and cummerbund.

Victorio & Lucchino

C. Sierpes, 87 (C2)
Showroom: C. Padre Luís María Llop
☎ 954 227 951
Open Mon.-Thurs. 9.15am-5.30pm, Fri. 9.15am-2pm.

you an idea of what a huge choice there actually is. Calzados Mayo also make made to measure dancing shoes and the famous *botas de Valverde* (Valverde boots) which aren't particularly feminine but are perfect for making the pilgrimage to El Rocío.

SILK EMBROIDERY

The secret skills involved in traditional embroidery have been passed down from generation to generation. Some of the techniques go back centuries and there are still some villages, such as Lagarta (Toledo) and Almadro (Ciudad Real) where this ancient art is still practised despite the introduction of machine embroidery and mass production. Fine needlecraft is now a cultural rarity and is very much a luxury product, but hand-embroidered fabrics still constitute an essential element in the trousseau of Seville's brides.

In this high fashion boutique run by two Sevillian designers, you can also find wedding outfits and *flamenca* dresses. Their collection brings a stunning touch of contemporary design to the traditional flamenco *traje de gitana* (gypsy girl's dress) and the dresses are so elegant that you're likely to want to wear them every day!

Barbara Quijano
C. Ximencz Enciso, 15 (C2)
☎ 954 228 524
Open every day 10am-8pm.

This little Aladdin's cave is easily recognised by its blue exterior. Inside is a treasure trove of flamenco dresses in avant-garde colours or with traditional polka-dot designs. The accessories, handbags and jewellery are also very pretty. You'll be particularly taken with the superb organdie shawls and positively knocked out by the beautiful cotton and silk scarves.

Calzados Mayo
Plaza del Alfalfa, 2 (C2)
☎/📠 954 225 555
**Open Mon.-Fri.
10am-1.30pm,
5-8.30pm, Sat.
10am-1.30pm.**
If you thought all flamenco shoes were the same then a visit to this shop will give

CHOOSE YOUR OWN *MANTILLA*

These days the *mantilla* (veil) is reserved for the more solemn occasions. Black ones are worn for sombre events such as Easter Week and funerals, while cream ones are worn at bullfights and weddings (apart, that is, from the mother of the groom who wears a black one). Protocol can be pretty strict – guests are only allowed to wear a *mantilla* when the marriage involves a member of the nobility. It's best to look closely at the invitation!

EMBROIDERY, SHAWLS AND *MANTILLAS*

Blasflor

C. Sierpes, 33 and 79 (C2)
☎ 954 227 661
Open Mon.-Fri. 10am-2pm, 5-8pm, Sat. 10am-2pm.

Blasflor specialises in traditional décor and there are several branches dotted around the city. The most popular stores, towards the centre of town, carry a wide range of gifts, decorative items and furniture.

They also have a fine selection of shawls for every budget, some made from pure silk, others from manmade fabrics. The most beautiful of the silk ones, embroidered with gold or silver thread, come from Manila. Don't get your heart too set on one though – it could set you back a tidy €600.

Artesania Textil

C. Sierpes, 70 (C2)
☎ 954 562 840
C. García de Venuesa, 33 (C3)
☎ 954 220 125
Open Mon.-Fri. 10am-2pm, 5-8pm, Sat. 10am-2pm.

Artesania Textil is a well-known luxury boutique which has been making and restoring handmade embroidery for over fifty years. They use only natural dyes in their silk embroidery and the techniques employed to restore items are over one hundred years old. The view here is that the traditional *mantilla* is an essential fashion accessory without which a woman is not fully dressed.

Bordados Foronda

C. Sierpes, 3 (C2)
☎ 954 227 661
Argote Molina, 20 (C2)
☎ 954 215 677
🖷 954 218 588
Open Mon.-Fri., 10am-2pm, 5-8pm, Sat. 10am-2pm.

Bordados Foronda is a shrine to handmade embroidery, where you can find something to suit all tastes. There's a full array of shawls and *mantillas* for the complete traditional Andalucian woman's ensemble. They also have dancing skirts and flamenco dresses, plus combs, fans and other accessories to go with them.

Juan Foronda

C. Tetúan, 28 (C3)
☎ 954 227 661
Open Mon.-Fri. 10.15am-
1.30pm, 4.30-8.30pm, Sat.
10.15am-2pm.

Juan Foronda is the official supplier of *mantillas* to the royal household. The company specialises in embroidery, including *mantones de manila*, which are magnificent hand-embroidered silk shawls. Prices are pretty high, but these are veritable treasures to be handed down as heirlooms from generation to generation.

Lenceria Interior

C. Rioja, 25 (C3)
☎ 954 224 437
Open Mon.-Fri. 10am-2pm,
5-8pm, Sat. 10am-2pm.

This shop specialises in embroidered lingerie and in brides' trousseaux. They will take orders for handmade bedspreads, curtains, pillowcases and table linen, and it goes without saying that nothing in traditional needlework is beyond them. The best quality is guaranteed so that you can order anything your heart desires in total confidence. If you fall in love with this shop, you'll also enjoy Lenceria Hogar (home furnishings), Plaza Manuel Alonso Vicedo, ☎ 954 214 630.

MUSIC AND DANCE ACCESSORIES

Artesanos Hermanos Hernandez

C. Léon XIII, 75 (A1-2)
☎ 954 387 101
Open Mon.-Fri. 10am-2pm,
5-8pm, Sat. 10am-2pm.

This shop draws professionals from the world of flamenco song and dance. The choice of castanets is astounding, with many different designs, sounds and prices. They are an interesting instrument and make wonderful souvenirs, but are very

difficult to play. Have a go yourself and see how many contrasting sounds these traditional Andalucian percussion instruments can produce.

Valeriano Bernal

Hernando del Pulgar, 20
(off map)
☎/℻ 954 582 679
or 630 444 905
www.valerianobernal.com

Even though Grenada's guitar makers normally win the prizes for the best flamenco guitars, this traditional classical and acoustic guitar shop is a perfect showcase for the talents of their Sevillian colleagues. A descendant of the classical and modern guitars that were developed in the 19th century, the flamenco guitar is lighter and

flatter and has a metal plate on which the musician beats out a rhythm. You can even try out an electric flamenco guitar. Tune one up and you can make believe you're famous guitarist Paco de Lucia, if only for a few minutes.

RECORDINGS

...dance of Andalucia will ... with the raw emotional power of its intoxicating beat. If you really want to submerge yourself in local culture, there's nothing better than getting out and about and sampling the sounds that form the very rhythm of the city's heartbeat. And if you want to take a little of the experience back with you, you could do worse than check out some of the bookshops and record stores.

around, as the cataloguing system is non-existent. However, the huge number of collector's items on offer makes you forget the mess and you'll soon be gleefully ferreting about among all the books, records, tapes and old cinema posters. You might find a real gem hidden amongst the traditional and popular recordings, from American hits of the 1960s to the very latest sounds.

Compas Sur Flamenco

Plaza de los Terceros, 10 (B2)
☎ 954 215 662
Open Mon.-Fri. 10am-2pm, 5-8pm, Sat. 10am-2pm.

Compas Sur Flamenco is well worth a visit if you want to take some of the sounds of flamenco back home with you and have a lasting memory of your trip to Seville. This well-stocked record shop is sure to have recordings that will appeal – they offer an irresistible choice of classical or modern flamenco music, rumbas and *sevillanas*.

Don Cecilio

C. Castilla, 47 (C4)
☎ 954 333 336
📠 954 333 294
Open Mon.-Fri. 10am-2pm, 5-8pm, Sat. 10am-2pm.

This little boutique in the heart of the Barrio de Triana buys and sells new and second-hand books and recordings. You can find almost anything here, especially if you like rummaging

Libreria Antonio Marchado

C. Alvarez Quintero, 5 (C2)
☎ 954 229 317
Open Mon.-Fri. 10am-2pm, 5-8pm, Sat. 10am-2pm.

This large cultural space, spread over two floors, is not just a bookshop, but a source of reference books covering the full

and tourist riches, whether in English, French or German, are generally pretty slight. Which is why you're reading this one!

Vértice

C. San Fernando, 33 (D2)
☎ 954 211 654
✆ 954 225 654
Open Mon.-Fri. 10am-2pm, 5-8pm, Sat. 10am-2pm.

This international bookshop located opposite the university has a wide selection of maps, guides, literary works

and novels about Seville that will help if you feel like delving deep into the city's soul. It also has a stock of the most important books on Seville by foreign writers. The service is straightforward and discreet and you'll be given ample time, space and peace in which to consult any works that particularly interest you.

gamut of Seville's arts and traditions. The dynamic owners also arrange cultural activities and artistic events throughout the year including book launches, private views, and art exhibitions.

Libreria Beta

Av. de la Constitución, 27 (C2-3/D2)
☎/✆] 954 560 703
Open Mon.-Fri. 10am-2pm, 5-8.30pm, Sat. 10am-2pm.

This bookshop, located down one side of the Puerta de Jerez, is very popular with tourists. As you'll soon realise, the city's Achilles heel is foreign languages — at every museum and historic building explanations are pretty rare in any language other than Spanish. The guides to Seville's historical

Allegro Música

C. Dos de Mayo, 38 (C3)
☎ 954 216 193
✆ 954 215 705
allegro@arrakis.es
Open Mon.-Fri. 10am-1.30pm, 5-8.30pm, Sat. 10am-2pm.

If you decide to take a part of the Andalucian experience home with you, then this music-lovers' paradise, just behind the Maestranza theatre, should be top of your list. Allegro Música offers the finest selection of Spanish and Arab-Andalucian music from flamenco to *zarzuela* (Spanish

musical theatre), on CD, cassette and DVD. To the background sounds of Spanish acoustic guitars, you can browse for Gregorian chant, symphonic, religious or baroque music. The staff are helpful and can offer advice in English, French or German — quite a rare occurrence in Seville, so enjoy it while you can!

Nightlife Practicalities

There's an element of magic about Seville after dark. Maybe the experience of the city is enhanced by the coolness of the night, which is so refreshing after the day's heat. Every evening, Sevillians set out on a mission to take over the streets and bars. There are endless options to choose from – the small, traditional tapas bars in Santa Cruz, the lively Alfalfa scene, or the romantic view over the Guadalquivir from the riverside bars in Triana. It's not difficult to find an excuse for not going to bed at all!

WHERE TO GO

You will have gathered that Sevillians enjoy their nightlife, so there are plenty of activities to suit a variety of tastes. You could start by visiting a few bars, or, if you prefer to dine at a restaurant, try going somewhere else for a drink afterwards. Whether you want to sit at a table or stand at the bar is another question for you to ponder. There are quiet places perfect for chatting, and lively bars if you feel like dancing. Alternatively you can relax in the al fresco bars that line the Guadalquivir or dance the night away at a nightclub. It's up to you. The choice of music is equally eclectic – pop, jazz, salsa and, of course, flamenco. It may be worth remembering that around September/October time, the best flamenco artists in the world.gather in Seville for the Bienal de Arte Flamenco.

GETTING AROUND

Next to each entry in the Shopping and Nightlife sections you'll find a map reference to help you find its location on the map on pp. 138–139.

WHERE TO GO FOR A NIGHT OUT

The city centre and the Barrio de Santa Cruz are extremely lively as they are choc-a-bloc with tapas bars. The open-air bars around the Alameda de

'CLASSIC' OUTINGS

Here are a few essential addresses:

Teatro Imperial
C. Sierpes, 25 (C2)
☎ 954 226 878
Privately owned repertory theatre giving a variety of productions.

Auditorio de la Cartuja
Isla de la Cartuja (B4)
☎ 954 464 148
Theatre, music and dance programmes.

La Imperdible
Plaza de San Antonio de Padua, 9 (B3)
☎ 954 388 219
Independent, very avant-garde theatre company.

Real Orquestra Sinfónica de Sevilla
(Royal Symphonic Orchestra of Seville)
C. Imagen, 9 (C2)
☎ 954 561 536
Classical music concerts and opera.

Iércules are the trendiest estinations for a few beers t the moment and Seville's ounger crowd tends to ongregate around the Plaza el Alfalfa. Last but not least, ou can spend a pleasant vening in Triana enjoying few drinks on the terrace f one of the bars that border ae Guadalquivir, while taking a the wonderful view of the ty across the river.

OPENING TIMES

ars start to liven up around m, when people meet up ter work. People tend to dine at around 10pm, either in a restaurant or by way of the famous *tapeo*, when they wander from bar to bar, sampling a little of the tapas in each. After around 11.30pm on weekdays, general drinking (or *copeo* as it is locally known) carries on until around midnight or 1am, when Sevillians tend to head off home. At the weekend there are no limits, and if you fancy getting on down in a club, don't arrive too early as the atmosphere doesn't really get going until after 2am.

CULTURAL EVENTS

In Seville there's a wide choice of concerts of both classical and flamenco music, as well as theatre and opera performances. The publication *Welcome & Olé*, freely available in hotels and Tourist Offices, can provide you with all the relevant details for this kind of entertainment. An even better bet is *El Giraldillo*, a monthly magazine which carries complete listings of the city's cultural events (www.elgiraldillo.es). It can be picked up free at most public buildings and from Tourist Offices. Information and tickets for major rock concerts are available at the **Sevilla Rock** music store
☎ 954 229 738.

HOW MUCH?

Going out in Seville needn't cost an arm and a leg. Most of the fun takes place in the streets or in bars, where entry is free. Drinks are for the most part not expensive, except in a few of the more exclusive places. Entry to a nightclub costs around €20, which includes a free drink.

WHAT TO WEAR

Sevillians, especially the women, like to dress up when they go out for a night on the town. Although there are no hard and fast rules as to what to wear in the bars, if you want to get into one of the more trendy clubs, you'll have to take a little more care over your presentation. Trainers are a definite no-no.

GETTING AROUND AT NIGHT

If your hotel is conveniently located (which means in easy walking distance of the city centre), you won't have much problem managing a night on the tiles on foot. There are plenty of bars, restaurants and other major nightspots all concentrated around the city centre. The only other effective and practical way of getting about is by taxi. Most journeys in the city will set you back around €4.

QUIET BARS

Café bar Abades

C. Abades, 13 (C2)
☎ 954 225 622
Open Mon. 9.30pm-dawn,
Tues.-Sat. 4pm-dawn, Sun.
4-8pm.

After a good dinner, it's a shame to waste the magic of a beautiful summer's evening and the excellent company you've been enjoying. Sometimes you just want to put the world to rights over a bottle of wine. Find a table outside on the terrace of the Abades Café and you can philosophise all night long. It's the perfect place either for a quiet discussion or a full-blown debate.

Café Sonanta

C. San Jacinto, 31 (C3/D3–4)
☎ 954 343 185
Open Mon.-Sat. 8.30am-
dawn, Sun. from 4pm.

It's quite tricky to know how to classify this café, as it serves breakfast in the morning, gradually transforms itself into a tapas bar during the day and finally ends up as a lively late-night bar. Whatever you want to call it, you can always get a drink here. It was finally decided to place it in the 'quiet bars' section because, like a lot of themed bars, it offers all sorts of cultural diversions on top of the usual service. There are flamenco concerts or theatrical shows every Thursday and art exhibitions displayed on the walls during the week.

LIVELIER BARS

Lo Nuestro

C. Betis, 31A (C3/D3)
Open every day from 10pm.

If you fancy a boogie to the seductive rhythms of the rumba, then try this bar, located on the popular and extremely lively Calle Betis, from 10pm onwards. While you sip your glass of *manzanilla* you can get a close look at flamenco dancing and may even be able to pluck up the courage to get out onto the dance floor and step to the beat of a *sevillana*!

Bar Adriano

C. Adriano, 5 (C3)
☎ 954 216 845
Open every day 10pm-6am.

This little bar certainly has a buzzing atmosphere, but it attracts a certain type of crowd. It's a real hotchpotch of tourist clichés – all revolving around bullfighting and flamenco. The only truly original part is the *rociero*, a corner dedicated to the cult of the Virgen del Rocío. The faithful gather here on occasion

to sing spontaneous songs of praise to their idol. Equally spontaneous are the impromptu concerts which occur when the guitar, which is usually kept behind the bar, finds its way into the hands of one of the locals who knows how to play a little

The resulting busking session can be very entertaining, so just go with the flow.

Antigüedades
C. Argote de Molina, 40 (C2)

This trendy bar is located on the ground floor of an old house. The owner lives on the floor above, but you should have no qualms about him spoiling the fun. He's a rather eccentric artist who spends most of his time running the bar. The décor is always highly original and changes according to the owner's whim. For example, don't be too surprised to find wicker bodies suspended from the ceiling.

La Fábrica
Plaza de Armas (B3)
Antigua Estación
☎ 954 908 828
www.lafabrica-cerveceros.com
Open every day noon-1am.

This bar, situated in an old railway station that has been converted into a shopping centre, sells beers from its own micro-brewery. You can try them out at one of the pleasant tables outside, perhaps along with some

Garlochi
C. Botero, 26 (C2)
Open every day 9pm-1am.

This little bar amalgamates the two opposing pillars of Seville's culture – festivals and religion. It almost feels sacrilegious to sit drinking 'the blood of Christ' in a room lined with relics and angelic statues. The walls are covered with hundreds of religious artefacts, giving the place a weird and dark atmosphere that has to be experienced to be believed.

delicious homemade food. The bar is open all day and you can sit and enjoy the ever-changing atmosphere as the evening approaches.

El Bulebar
Alameda de Hércules, 83
☎ 954 901 954
Open every day 1pm-1am.

This bar has recently become one of the trendiest drinking places in Seville. Almost hidden by the plethora of bars surrounding it, this rather original establishment is almost like two bars in one. Inside, you can dance your socks off to great music, with

live concerts on Wednesdays, while outside you can sit in a completely different atmosphere of relative tranquillity – and get your breath back.

TABLAOS – ANDALUCIAN CABARET SHOWS

Los Gallos
Plaza de Santa Cruz, 11 (C2)
☎ 954 216 981.

Set right in the heart of Santa Cruz, Los Gallos is almost a tradition in itself. Their *tablao* stages some of the best flamenco singing and dancing in the city.

There's a choice of two shows every day, the first between 9 and 11pm and the second between 11.30pm and 1.30am.

El Arenal

C. Rodo, 7 (C3)
☎ 954 216 492
📠 954 210 468
www.tablaoelarenal.com

This traditional flamenco show takes place in a 17th-century building. Tickets cost €29 including a drink or €57 if you want to have dinner as well. There are two shows starting at 9.30pm and 11.30pm.

Casa de la Memoria de Al-Andalus

C. Ximénez Enciso, 28 (C2)
☎/📠 954 560 670
Concert daily at 9pm.
Centre open every day 9am-2.30pm and 6.30pm until the end of the concert.
Temporary exhibitions open 10am-2.30pm and 6.30pm until the end of the concert.

This centre, dedicated to the preservation of Andalucian history and folklore as a living tradition, organizes a variety of events including exhibitions, lectures and concerts. Every Thursday, Saturday and Sunday they stage a flamenco show. If you're in the Barrio de Santa Cruz, pop in and pick up a programme for full details of their season of events.

El Simpecao

C. Castilla, 82 (C4)
Open every day from 10pm.

Triana, if you hadn't already realised it, is one of the homes of flamenco, but there's much more to this bar than that. It aims to cater to a variety of moods. One room is devoted to bullfighting, another has a markedly religious theme.

The cabaret involves either a variety of improvised performances, or a show given by *grupos rocieros* (Rocío groups) who perform songs in praise of the Virgen del Rocío. You're encouraged to join in with their singing and dancing. El Simpecao also has a pretty terrace, which is a perfect spot to enjoy hot summer nights.

CABARETS, JAZZ AND SHOWS

La Carbonería
C. Levíes, 18 (C2)
☎ 954 214 460
Open every day 7pm-3am.

This venue, located in an old charcoal factory, is great if you can't make up your mind. Jazz lovers can listen in the comfort of a huge room with an enormous fireplace. If you prefer flamenco, there's another room, resembling a school dining room, where everyone sits together at long tables with a

counter down each side – one serving tapas, the other drinks. The tapas are nothing special except for the *chorizo al infierno* (very hot sausage) which you have to cook before eating. If it's too hot for you, you can cool off at one of the tables outside.

El Aviador
Ronda de Triana s/n (C4/D4)
☎ 954 332 586
Open every day 3pm-3am.

One of the liveliest bars in the city with great music (jazz, blues and more up-to-date sounds). The name means 'the Aviator' and as you'd expect, the décor is aviation-oriented.

La Cara B
Bustos Tavera, 13 (B2)
Open from 9pm.

This bar has the atmosphere of a cavern club, and features some fantastic music including rock, blues, grunge and new wave. One of the most exciting venues in the city, it quickly gained a reputation as being one of *the*

certainly be blown away by the size of the place, with its four bars, each with a different themed décor. It also has a superbly equipped dance arena playing a variety of music styles throughout the night.

Holiday

Jesús del Gran Poder, 73 (B3)
☎ 954 379 655
Open Thurs.-Sat. 10pm-5am,
Sun. 6pm-1am.

This is probably Seville's biggest and most modern nightclub. The eclectic music and atmosphere will keep you dancing until the small hours.

CLASSICAL MUSIC AND THEATRE

Teatro Central

Isla de la Cartuja s/n (B4)
☎ 954 460 780
or 954 460 600
❶ 954 460 880
www.teatrocentral.com
Admission €9-12.

Built on the island of La Cartuja by the banks of the Guadalquivir, this modern theatre bears witness to Seville's rich cultural heritage of theatre, flamenco, contemporary dance, jazz, etc. It seats between 390 and 900 spectators depending on the production and the configuration of the auditorium.

places to hang out in Seville. The drink prices are subject to various promotional offers, but only up until midnight, so keep an eye on the clock. It's also a great place to shoot a few games of pool.

CLUBS

El Coto

Av. Luis Montoto, 118 (C1)
☎ 954 571 072
Open every day
Admission €18

Located in the Meliá Los Lebreros hotel, this is one of the city's trendiest nightspots and is popular with Seville's chic in-crowd. It's a great place for an all-night experience – if you can last the pace.

Boss

C. Betis, 67 (C3/D3)
Open Thurs.-Sun. 8pm-7am.

Despite changing hands a number of times, this club has always managed to retain its fashionable status. You will

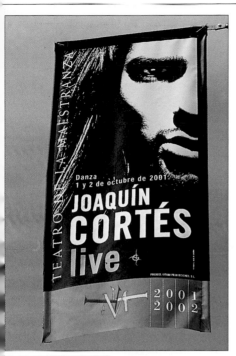

This is one of Spain's principal venues for opera and symphony concerts, and was equipped with all the very latest technology during a recent restoration. If you get the chance, try to get to see a *zarzuela*, which is a Spanish operetta. Their website, although in Spanish, should give you a good idea of their programme and prices

Teatro Lope de Vega

Av. de María Luisa (D2)
☎ 954 590 853
or 954 590 827
(Information only. Bookings cannot be made over the phone.)
Box office open every day 11am-2pm, 6-9pm.
Admission €6-15 for theatre, €9-21 for other events.

Built for the 1929 World Exhibition, the Lope de Vega theatre is situated next to the Parque de María Luisa. It stages a varied programme of 'classical' theatre taken from a wide repertory, which in Seville naturally includes flamenco music and dance.

Teatro de la Maestranza

Paseo de C. Colón, 22 (D3)
☎ 954 223 344
☎ 954 226 573 (tickets)

www.maestranza.com
Box office: Open every day, 10am-2pm, 6-9pm.
Admission €16-70 for opera, €10-50 for classical concerts and dance.

Don't miss...

Here is a selection of 12 of the most beautiful sites in Seville that should be on any visitor's list.

1 THE CATHEDRAL

The essential monument if you really want to appreciate virtually every facet of Seville's art and history.

2 IGLESIA DE SANTA ANA

The oldest church in Seville is an impressive historical monument but also contains one or two amusing curiosities.

3 MONASTERIO SAN CLEMENTE

A place of worship, museum, bakery and pottery workshop in one – this monastery is certainly good value.

4 HOSPITAL DE LA CARIDAD

One of the most striking and impressive buildings in the city, full of works of art by Murillo and Valdés Leal.

5 MUSEO DE BELLAS ARTES

The fine art museum houses an authoritative collection of Spanish and Andalucian art, from early medieval painting to the Seville school of the Golden Age.

6 EL ALCAZAR

Breathtaking interiors, courtyards and gardens combine to enchanting effect in a highlight of Seville's awesome heritage.

7 El Ayuntamiento

Head off to the town hall and try to solve the riddle of the
'NO do' (see p. 128).

8 The University

What connects Spanish cigars
with this seat of learning?
It was once the tobacco factory
where 'Carmen' worked.

9 La Maestranza

Unending passion, flamenco,
tapas ... and bulls and *toreros*
of course. Bullfighting is more
than just a blood sport, as a
visit here will reveal.

10 Casa de Pilatos

The full glory of the city's
Roman and Italian past can be
seen in this graceful mansion,
which combines Mudéjar,
Gothic and Renaissance styles.

11 Palacio Lebrija

This exquisite collection of
treasures, housed in beautiful,
elegant surroundings, testifies
to the taste and finesse of the
Countess of Lebrija.

12 Parque de María Luisa

Seville has everything – even a vast expanse of open green space
in the very heart of the city. Romance and relaxation for all.

1 The Cathedral

Seville's majestic Gothic cathedral, built on the former site of the Great Mosque, receives record numbers of visitors. The third largest cathedral in the world, it offers a glimpse into the heart of a past rich in art and history. A stroll through its five naves, past the richly decorated chapels, reveals examples of works by Zurbarán, Luis de Vargas and Murillo amongst others.

EL PATIO DE LOS NARANJOS

You can reach this picturesque courtyard, planted with orange trees, either from outside via the Puerta del Perdón or from the cathedral through the former sacristy. The cathedral entrance, the Puerta del Lagarto (lizard door) contains a wooden crocodile, a replica of the one presented to Alfonso X by the Sultan of Egypt when he came to ask for his daughter's hand in marriage.

LA CAPILLA MAYOR

The Capilla Mayor contains one of the world's most significant works of religious

art – the massive Gothic altarpiece for the high altar designed by Pieter Dankart in 1482. Measuring 220 sq m (2,400 sq ft), it took teams of highly skilled sculptors until 1525 to complete. Its 36 gilded and sculpted sections depict stories from the Old Testament and the life of Christ.

THE TOMB OF CHRISTOPHER COLUMBUS

At the far end of the transept, near the San Cristóbal door, four figures, representing the kingdoms of Navarre, Castile, León and Aragon, support the tomb of the explorer Christopher Columbus. His remains were brought back to Seville from Havana in 1898, when Spanish rule over Cuba came to an end.

LA CAPILLA REAL

The richly-decorated Capilla Real (Royal Chapel) contains the Virgen de los Reyes (Virgin of the Kings), a Gothic icon of the French school, said to have been presented by St Louis, King of France, to his cousin Fernando III, King of

Castile. Below the Virgin is a silver urn, which according to legend contains the uncorrupted body of the saintly king, San Fernando.

The tomb of Christopher Columbus

INFORMATION

The Cathedral
(see p. 36)
Plaza Virgen de los Reyes
(enter via the Puerta del Oriente)
☎ 954 214 971
or 954 563 321
🖷 954 564 743
Open Mon.-Sat. 11am-5pm, Sun. 2-6pm (these times may be subject to change).
Entry charge, free on Sun.

2 Iglesia de Santa Ana

This beautifully proportioned church is popularly held to be Triana's very own cathedral. Believed to be the oldest church in Seville, it was founded by Alfonso X (the Wise) in the 1260s in gratitude for the healing of an eye affliction. It has endured various alterations over the centuries, the most significant after an earthquake in 1755.

Pila de los Gitanos

Jurate and Nufro Ortega. The central sculpture group represents St Anne with the Virgin and Child. Scattered throughout the church are 24 panels by various artists, dating from 1557. They depict scenes from the lives of St Anne, St Joseph and the Virgin. The main chapel contains a number of interesting altarpieces, including a wooden relief of St Jerome which is attributed to Torrigiano.

THE EXTERIOR

The construction of the building took place at the interface between the Gothic and Romanesque styles. One of the most important modifications to the building was made in 1755, after the terrible earthquake that destroyed Lisbon. The tower an afterthought, added to the original, which still retains elements of its 14th-century Mudéjar origins at its lower extremities. The two upper parts are decorated with blue Renaissance-period tiles.

THE ALTARPIECES

The main nave is dominated a superb Renaissance altarpiece, the work of Nicolás

SOME CURIOS AND MASTERPIECES

In the left-hand nave you'll find an altar with representations of St Justa

and St Rufina, both dressed in 18th-century costume, while in the right-hand nave is a wonderful polyptych of St Catalina painted by Hernando de Stumio in 1553. Just above it, you can see one of the most curious works of art in the church – a tomb by Niccolo Pisano, decorated with *azulejos*. It shows the body of a recumbent man, dressed in yellow with long green socks and black shoes. Also take a look at the impressive silver monstrance, which was made by Mateo Ximenes in the 17th century.

INFORMATION

Iglesia de Santa Ana
(see p. 60)
Calle Pureza, 84
☎ 954 271 382
Open every day 9-11am,
7-9pm.
Free entry.

3 Monasterio de San Clemente

T his monastery, founded by Alfonso X (the Wise), was once used as a summer residence by the Moorish kings. Today it's used as an exhibition space, though nuns still live here, dedicating themselves to the art of pastry-making. The monastery church has some interesting works of art as well as a pretty cloister, which dates from the 17th century.

THE CHURCH

Richly decorated in a number of styles dating from the 13th to the 18th century, the Mudéjar *artesonado* (panelled) ceiling is particularly wonderful, as are the stunning 16th-century *azulejo* tiles and the frescoes by Valdés Leal, including *The Entry of King San Fernando into Seville*.

THE ALTARPIECES

As well as a superb main altarpiece from 1640 by Felipe de Rivas, there's also a beautiful 1248 example known as *La Virgen del Rey* (the King's Virgin). It forms part of the *Fernandina* collection of works, donated by King San Fernando III to several churches in Seville to encourage the growth of Christianity.

THE ROYAL PANTHEON

The church was used as a royal burial ground for many years. The main chapel contains the tomb of Queen María of Portugal, widow of King Alfonso XI and mother of Pedro I. Covered in red damask and a royal crown,

the tomb is decorated with a remarkable tile-work design. Outside, down the side of the wall, a tiled plaque explains the history of the convent.

THE TOMB OF DOÑA MARIA

A tragic story links María of Portugal to the convent. Doña María was refused the honour of being buried in the Royal Chapel in the cathedral as she spent a large part of her lifetime plotting against her own son, Pedro the Cruel. She took not only his crown, but his life as well.

INFORMATION

Monasterio de San Clemente (see p. 55)
Calle Reposo, 9
☎ 954 379 905
Convent church:
Open Mon.-Sat. 6-9pm, Sun. and public holidays noon-2pm.
Handmade pastries and ceramics: shop open 10am-1pm, 4-6pm.
Free entry.

4 Hospital de la Caridad

Blessed with an extraordinary radiance which worked to calm and relax both the bodies and spirits of its elderly patients, the hospital's exterior is decorated with delicate, tile-work designs painted by Murillo. Inside, two quiet and peaceful courtyards lead to the hospital's pride and joy – the chapel of Señor San Jorge.

The Miracle of the Loaves and Fishes, located opposite each other. There are also tenderly painted pictures of *The Infant Jesus* and *St John the Baptist as a child.*

ALTARPIECES AND SCULPTURES

The church also contains some beautiful baroque sculptures including *The Virgin of Charity*, *St Joseph* and an *Ecce Homo* or *Kneeling Christ*. The main altarpiece, the most important work of art in the church, is a masterpiece of Spanish baroque. This structure is the work of Bernardo Simón de Pineda, while the paintings and gilding are by Valdés Leal and the sculptures by Pedro Roldán. The central grouping depicts Christ being laid in his tomb.

Valdés Leal, Finis Gloriae Mundi

LESSON IN LIFE AND DEATH

The interior of the hospital is decorated according to a specific iconographic plan laid down by its founder, Miguel Mañara, who was saved from a dissolute life by a dream in which he foresaw his own death. As you enter, be prepared for the sight of two deeply disturbing pictures by Valdés Leal. The one on the right depicts Judgement Day, with Christ weighing up the sinners and the virtuous on a pair of scales. On the left, is a depiction of the victory of death over life and the futility

of material riches – a priest who has enjoyed a wealthy life is nothing more than food for worms as he lies in his coffin.

FROM VALDÉS LEAL TO MURILLO

Several paintings by Murillo decorate the walls and the numerous altarpieces. Two of them, *St John of God carrying a sick man* and *St Elizabeth of Hungary caring for the afflicted,* allude to one of the most important activities of the hospital brotherhood – care of the sick. There are two further remarkable pictures to admire: *Moses striking the rock* and

INFORMATION

Hospital de la Caridad (see p. 47)
Calle Temprado, 3
☎ 954 223 232
Open Mon.-Sat. 9am-1.30pm, 3.30-6.30pm,
Sun. and public holidays 9am-1pm.
Entry charge.

5 Museo de Bellas Artes

It's worth spending some time in this distinguished museum, housed in the former Convento de la Merced. Behind the exterior, with its depiction of *The Virgin of Mercy*, there are currently 14 galleries set around three cloisters, displaying masterworks of Spanish art and medieval sculpture from Seville.

CONVENTO DE LA MERCED

Founded by St Pietro Nolasco and built between 1600 and 1612 by Juan de Oviedo, this was one of the Church's greatest and richest convents in the 16th and 17th centuries. It was funded by donations from families who devoted themselves to ransoming prisoners and hostages from North African pirates.

THE GROUND FLOOR

Here you can see some early examples of Seville's medieval art on display, including Pedro Millán's sculpture *Christ being placed in the tomb* in Room I

and Alejo Fernández's *Annunciation* in Room II.

THE FIRST FLOOR

This floor is dedicated to Seville's baroque movement. You can see some stunning depictions of the Virgin by Murillo and his pupils in Room VII and, in Room VIII, a display dedicated to Valdés Leal with religious paintings such as *La Immaculada* (The Immaculate Virgin) and *La Flagelación* (The Scourging).

ROOM X

This room displays works by Zurbarán, including the monumental *San Hugo en el Refectorio* (St Hugh in the Refectory), the votive image of the *Virgen de las Cuevas* (Virgin of the Caves), painted in 1655, and his masterpiece, *The Apotheosis of St Thomas Aquinas* (1631).

Murillo, Santa Justa y Rufina

INFORMATION

Museo Bellas Artes (see p. 56)
Plaza del Museo, 9
☎ **954 220 790**
or 954 221 829
ⓕ 954 224 324
www.junta-andalucia.es/cultura
Open Tues. 3-8pm, Weds.-Sat. 9am-8pm, Sun. and public holidays 9am-3pm.
Free entry for EU citizens.

Zurbarán, The Virgin of the Cav

THE CHURCH

The former convent church can be reached through the main cloister. This old chapel with its superb dome painted by Domingo Martínez, has become the museum's main exhibition room. It contains works mostly with a religious theme, in keeping with the setting, most notably a group of 17th-century masterpieces by artists from the Seville school with some wonderful examples by Murillo.

6 El Alcázar

Once the palace of Spain's first kings, this gem has been declared a UNESCO world heritage site. From its early foundations in 844, of which only an Almohad wall and the Patio del Yeso (plasterwork courtyard) remain, the Mudéjar craftsmen stayed true to its Islamic heritage, under the orders of Alfonso X and later Pedro the Cruel.

PALACIO DE CARLOS V

Carlos V's personal apartments are decorated in the mannerist style, with ornate 16th-century tiles and superb tapestries decorating the walls. In the Great Hall there are some more wonderful tapestries from Flanders, depicting the fall of Tunis.

PATIO DE LAS DONCELAS

According to tradition, the ladies of the court would gather in the Patio de las Doncelas (maiden's courtyard) to spend time together. Surrounded by marble columns, it is decorated with stucco foliage in the Moorish style as well as Christian coats of arms and inscriptions.

Don't forget to look up to admire the panelled ceilings, decorated with inlaid wood and 14th-century *azulejo* tiles.

SALON DE EMBAJADORES

The Hall of the Ambassadors is best known for its impressive cupola, created by the Sevillian artist Diego Ruiz in 1389. Made in Moorish style of carved cedarwood, in a shape known as *media naranja* (half-orange), it's decorated with gold stucco and tiny light-reflecting mirrors.

PATIO DE LA MONTERÍA

Gentlemen and beaters accompanying the king on his hunting parties would gather in the Patio de la Montería (the

INFORMATION

El Alcazar
(see p. 39)
Patio de Banderas
☎ **954 502 323**
www.patronato-
alcazarsevilla.es
Open Tue.-Sat. 9.30am-
7pm, Sun. 9.30am-5pm.
Entry charge.

hunting party's courtyard). It's a typical example of a *mechouar*, a characteristic element of Muslim households, which is an area designed to separate private buildings from the public gaze.

THE GARDENS

The gardens were redesigned by Carlos V and include Arabic, French and Renaissance styles. Each garden has its own name and history – the Prince's garden, the Ladies' garden, with its mock caves and fountains, the hedged Labyrinth (*Laberinto*), first laid down in the 17th century, and the mannerist-style Estanque (pond) garden.

7 El Ayuntamiento

Seville's town hall is flanked by two places of great historic significance. On one side lies the Plaza de San Francisco, site of autos-da-fe ('acts of faith') during the Inquisition, when huge crowds would gather to witness the fate of those indicted for heresy. On the other side (now the Plaza Nueva), stood the monastery of San Francisco where monks bound for the New World were trained.

LA FACHADA DEL RELOJ

The town hall was built on the orders of Carlos V on the occasion of his wedding in the ancient city of Hispalis. The plans were drawn up by architect Diego de Riaño in adherence to the strict rules of pure Renaissance style. The very sombre *fachada del reloj* (clock frontage) is from the 19th century, when it was decided to demolish the monastery of San Francisco to create the Plaza Nueva.

AROUND THE PLAZA DE SAN FRANCISCO

You could spend hours gazing at the hundreds of intricately detailed sculptures on the finely-carved plateresque (early Renaissance decoration) façade which faces the Plaza de San Francisco. The beauty of the *Arquillo del Ayuntamiento*, a stunningly carved, arched gate, which was once the entrance to the town hall, is particularly striking.

'NO DO'

On the same façade, you'll see a coat of arms bearing the words 'NO' and 'Do'. If you look carefully, you'll also spot it in several other places in the building, as well as around the city in general. It is actually the coat of arms conferred on Seville by King Alfonso X the Wise in gratitude for the city's support during his battles against his son. Between the two words, 'NO' and 'Do', lies a bundle of wool (*madeja* in Spanish). If you link these three elements together, you end up with an approximation of the Spanish expression *no me ha dejado*, meaning 'they (the people) did not abandon me'.

THE INTERIOR

The building's interior is a hotchpotch of Gothic and Renaissance styles. On the ground floor there's a council meeting room, a rather ostentatious space with an extraordinary coat of arms by the sculptor Roque de Balduque. The ceiling is covered with busts of different Spanish kings.

INFORMATION

El Ayuntamiento (see p. 42)
Plaza Nueva, 1
☎ 954 590 101
Open Tues.-Thurs.
5.30-6.30pm, Sat.
11.30am-12.30pm
Closed from 15 July
to 15 Sept.

8 The University

The University of Seville has gathered its faculties of law, philology, history and geography under one enormous roof and this historic building, littered with courtyards and fountains, is open to the public. The architecture is in the florid style of the 18th century, which was perfectly suited to such grand designs as this former Seville tobacco factory, which was completed in 1771 and formed the backdrop to Bizet's opera *Carmen*.

THE HISTORY OF ITS CONSTRUCTION

The world's first tobacco factory was originally built in the Plaza del Cristo de Burgos. Fernando VI, feeling that the building was not big enough, ordered the construction of a new, more modern factory, designed on a massive scale. The project was initially entrusted to a military engineer, Ignacio Sala, who eventually gave way to architects Johannes van den Berg – who was responsible for the moat surrounding the university – Vincente Catalán and Bengoechea. Construction was interrupted several times and the building was not completed until 1771.

INFORMATION

La Universidad
(see p. 48)
Calle San Fernando, 4
☎ 954 551 000
**Open Mon.-Fri.
8am-8.30pm.
Free entry.**

THE CALLE SAN FERNANDO FAÇADE

The main gate of this impressive 250 m (273 yd) long façade was designed by architect Johannes van den Berg. It is neo-Classical in style and is decorated with royal coats of arms and the busts of two important historical figures – Christopher Columbus and Hernán Cortes, the latter an incorrigible smoker. If you look up to the top of the pediment, you'll see a charming statue of Fame surrounded by lilies, sounding a trumpet.

THE SMUGGLER'S PRISON

A lot of care had to be taken by the tobacco business to protect its products from theft. The factory therefore included a security system comprising 300 m (328 yds) of moat, a drawbridge and sentry boxes. The complex also had its own prison, located to the right of the main entrance, which was used as late as the 19th century to lock up employees who were tempted to try their hand at tobacco smuggling.

9 La Maestranza

The Maestranza bullfighting arena is one of the definitive symbols of the city. It belongs to the Real Maestranza de Caballería de Sevilla, a noble body with a long and proud history. Originally built in 1761 under the direction of Pedro and Vincente San Martín, the building was restored to its former glory in the 20th century.

The stables

AN EXTRAORDINARY EDIFICE

The strong contrast between the subdued architecture of the late baroque-style exterior and the profusion of decoration inside is immediately noticeable. La Maestranza is distinguished by the oval shape

The chapel

of its arena, which is surrounded by two banks of terraced seating. The first, lower section is open to the elements whilst the upper section is protected by a columned gallery. The higher you go, the more you are shielded from the sun – and the more expensive the seats.

LA PUERTA DEL PRÍNCIPE

The arena's main façade fronts the Paseo de Cristóbal Colón, and this is where you can see the famous Puerta del Príncipe. The gateway is constructed from marble and the wrought iron gates were originally made in the 17th century by Pedro Roldán for a convent that has long since disappeared. Above the Puerta del Príncipe,

you can see the Royal box, which is covered by a vaulted ceiling decorated with blue and white tiles.

FROM THE CHAPEL TO THE INFIRMARY

Inside the arena, there are three more gates – the bulls enter through the Puerta de Toriles and, after the coup de grâce, they are dragged away through the Puerta de Arrastre (dragging gate). The Puerta de Enfermería leads to the infirmary. A guided tour takes you round the arena and includes the museum, the infirmary, the stables and the chapel.

INFORMATION

La Maestranza
(see p. 46)
Paseo de Colón, 12
☎ 954 224 577
Open every day 9.30am-2pm, 3-7pm except on bullfight days when visits are only until 3pm (excluding chapel and stables).
Entry charge.

10 Casa de Pilatos

This sumptuous palace, built by the first Marqués de Tarifa in the 16th century, is the starting point for the Way of the Cross procession, which sets off on Good Friday. From here the pilgrims make their way to the church of Cruz del Campo just outside the city, covering the same distance as the route from Mount Golgotha to the house of Pontius Pilate in Jerusalem, after which the Casa de Pilatos is named.

IN HOMAGE TO...

A beautiful Italianate balcony dominates the exterior of the palace. It is decorated with two heraldic shields, one displaying the coat of arms of the Ribera family and the other an image of the Holy Sepulchre, created to commemorate a pilgrimage to Jerusalem by Don Fadrique Enríquez in 1520.

central fountain are the work of the Aprile family, who were well-known Italian artists.

ROMAN SCULPTURES

Today the palace houses a fine collection of Roman statuary. A large selection of busts of Roman Emperors as well as of classical writers and characters from mythology can be seen in the courtyard and throughout the ground floor.

THE COURTYARD

The inner courtyard is simply majestic. Surrounded by Mudéjar arches, it contains two magnificent statues of Athena, one armed for war, the other at peace, both copied from original works by Phidias. The pillars and the

THE GRAND STAIRCASE AND THE ART COLLECTIONS

A magnificent staircase, decorated with *azulejos* and covered by a spectacular

golden dome, leads to the first floor. The ornate rooms house a fine collection of Chinese porcelain, examples of Mudéjar decorative art and a collection of paintings from the Italian and Flemish schools, as well as a handsome ceiling, illustrating the Apotheosis of Hercules, the work of Francisco Pacheco in 1603.

INFORMATION

Casa de Pilatos
(see p. 43)
Plaza de Pilatos, 1
☎ **954 225 298**
Open daily, 9am-7pm;
July-Sept. 9am-8pm
(closed Mon., Thur., Sat.
in Aug.)
Entry charge.

11 Palacio Lebrija

This beautiful mansion, dating from the 16th century and located in the centre of the city, is typically Sevillian, and was restored to its former glory in 1914, thanks to the Condesa de Lebrija. The entrance is through a huge iron gate, which protects a magnificent studded mahogany door. Inside, the palace boasts some stunning archaeological treasures including some superb Roman mosaics, which have made it one of the most important private collections in the world.

THE GROUND FLOOR

It's here you'll find Lebrija palace's famous mosaics. The one adorning the main courtyard is huge and in excellent condition. The Medusa and Ganymede rooms contain scenes depicting their mythological namesakes and the Hermes room is full of treasures found in the nearby Roman city of Itálica. Last but not least, the *Cenador de Cristal* (glass dining room) is a charming vaulted room which leads out to the garden, where you'll find a wall covered in 15th-century tiles originating from the San Agustín convent.

in Triana. The banisters are made from mahogany, the steps of marble, and if you look up, you'll see a magnificent Mudéjar-style ceiling.

THE FIRST FLOOR

On the first floor, you'll find works of art from every period arranged with the characteristic elegance and style of the Condesa de Lebrija. The amazing ceiling in the dining room, decorated with porcelain plaques, may even render you speechless. Successive rooms, decorated in baroque, Arabian and Empire styles, each display art treasures appropriate to their décor theme.

INFORMATION

Palacio Lebrija
(see p. 44)
Calle Cuna, 8
☎ 954 218 183
🖷 954 501 029
www.palaciodelebrija.com
Open Mon.-Fri.
10.30am-1pm, 5-7.30pm
(4.30-7pm in winter),
Sat. 10am-1pm.
Entry charge.

THE STAIRCASE

A sumptuous staircase leads up to the first floor. Typically Sevillian in design, it's entirely covered with 16th- and 17th-century tiles, painted locally

12 Parque de María Luisa

This park bears witness to the wonderful talents of Moorish landscape artists. Situated right in the heart of the city, this huge garden, bordered by wide boulevards, is superbly laid out. There's nothing like a stroll through the Parque de María Luisa's peaceful and lush environment to calm the senses.

THE 1929 PAVILIONS

Set within and around the edges of the park are a number of pavilions built for the Iberian–American Exhibition of 1929. If you walk down the Avenida de la Palmera, you can see how the participating countries – Chile, Peru, Mexico, Guatemala and Colombia – all vied with each other to build their national pavilions in the most elegant style.

LA PLAZA DE ESPAÑA

The buildings on the Plaza de España are highly representative of Andalucian architecture, mixing marble, brick and *azulejos* in typical regional style. Designed to house the offices of the 1929 Exhibition, they now contain local-government offices and the general headquarters of the regional armed forces.

THE ROYAL PAVILION

Like the rest of the buildings in the Plaza de América, this neo-Gothic pavilion was designed by Anibal González. It now forms part of the Junta de Andalucía (Andalucian government) and isn't open to the public, but the exterior can still be admired.

MUSEO ARQUEOLÓGICO

The archaeological museum, housed in a neo-Renaissance building, is considered to be

one of the most beautiful in Spain. It contains remarkable collections of prehistoric and Visigoth artefacts as well as some notable statues from Itálica – one of Spain's major Roman cities, located 13 km (8 miles) north of Seville.

MUSEO DE ARTES Y COSTUMBRES POPULARES

Housed in the Mudéjar pavilion of the Plaza de América, this museum of folklore and arts displays various collections of traditional Andalucian objects, including costumes, jewellery and bullfighting accessories, along with all the typical outfits associated with Seville's festivals and customs.

More handy words and phrases

Don't assume that everyone in Seville will speak English. Although multilingual people are often employed in places that deal with tourists, this is by no means the norm. More Handy Words and Phrases can be found on the back flap of the cover.

USEFUL EXPRESSIONS

Can you speak more slowly, please?
¿Puede hablar mas despacio, por favor?

Could you repeat that please?
¿Podría repetirlo por favor?

I don't speak Spanish
No hablo español

Do you understand?
¿Me entiende?

I am sorry
Lo siento/Disculpe

Is it possible...?
¿Sería posible…?

My name is…
Me llamo…

What is your name?
¿Como se llama?

Pleased to meet you
Encantado/a (m/f)

How are you?
¿Qué tal?

Fine, thank you
Muy bien, gracias

Who?
¿Quien?

Why?
¿Porqué?

How?
¿Cómo?

What is it?
¿Qué es?

Here
Aqui

There
Allá

Slow
Lento

Fast
Rápido

Another
Otra vez

Near
Cerca

Good
Bueno

Bad
Malo

Big
Grande

Small
Pequeno

Hot
Caliente

Cold
Frío

Free (no charge)
Gratis

Free (unoccupied)
Desocupado

Busy (occupied)
Ocupado

Toilets/WC
Baño *or* aseos

No smoking
No fumar

AT THE HOTEL

Do you have a room for one person/for two people?
¿Tiene una habitación para una persona/para dos personas?

A quiet room
Una habitación tranquila

With a bath
Con baño

With shower
Con ducha

Bed
Cama

Key
Llave

Lift
El ascensor

First floor
El primer piso

Second floor
El segundo piso

IN THE TOWN

What time does it open/close?
¿A qué hora abre/cierra?

I would like to go…
Quisiera ir…

Is it far/near?
¿Está lejos/cerca?

Straight on
Todo recto

At the end of
Al final de

Next to
Al lado de

Opposite
Frente a

Above
Sobre

Below
Debajo

Up
Arriba

Down
Abajo

Entrance
Entrada

Exit
Salida

Post
Correo

Letter
Carta

Envelope
Sobre

Stamp
Sello

Map of the city
Mapa de la ciudad

Art gallery
Galería de arte

Castle
Castillo

Cathedral
Catedral

Church
Iglesia

Museum
Museo

News-stand
Kiosco de revistas

Park
Jardin

Square
Plaza

Town hall
Ajuntemiento

TRAVEL
Timetable
Horario

By plane/train/car
Por avión/tren/coche

Airport
Aeropuerto

**Do I need to change
platforms?**
Debo cambiar de plataforma?

**What platform does it
leave from?**
De qué plataforma sale?

Railway station
Estación de tren

Underground
Metro

Bus
Autobus

A ticket to…
Un billete para…

Single/return
Ida/ida y vuelta

Bicycle
Bicicleta

On foot
A pie

AT THE RESTAURANT
**What's the dish
of the day?**
¿Cual es el plato del dia?

**What's the house
specialty?**
¿Cual es la especialidad
de la casa?

I am a vegetarian
Soy vegetariano/a

DRINKS
Coffee
Café

Lemonade
Limonada

Orange juice
Zumo de naranja

Red/white
Tinto/blanco

Sherry
Jerez

Sparkling wine
Cava

Still/sparkling
Sin gas/con gas

Tea
Té

SUNDRIES
Egg
Huevo

French fries
Patatas fritas

Fruit
Fruta

Mustard
Mostaza

Oil
Aceite

Omelette
Tortilla

Rice
Arroz

Sandwich
Bocadillo

Sauce
Salsa

Soup
Sopa

Spicy
Picante

Sugar
Azúcar

Vegetables
Legumbres

Vinegar
Vinagre

MEAT AND FISH
Rare
Poco hecho

Medium
Termino medio

Well-done
Bien cocido

Beef
Vaca

Chicken
Pollo

Duck
Pato

Fish
Pescado

Ham
Jamón

Lamb
Cordero

Oysters
Ostras

Pork
Cochino/puerco

Sausage
Chorizo/embutido

Shrimp
Langostino/gamba

Squid
Pulpo

SHOPPING
I would like to buy
Quisiera comprar

Where can I find...?
¿Dónde puedo encontrar...?

Do you have?
¿Tiene?

Small
Pequeña

Medium
Mediana

Large
Grande

Smaller
Más pequeño

Bigger
Más grande

Belt
Cinturón

Book
Libro

Boot
Lota

Boxer shorts
Calzoncillos

Bracelet
Pulsera, bracelete

Checked pattern
Cuadros

Coat
Abrigo

Cotton
Algodón

Dress
Vestido

Earrings
Pendientes

Furniture
Muebles

Gold
Oro

Handbag
Bolso

Hat
Sombrero

Jacket
Chaqueta (men),
Americana (women)

Jewel
Joya

Leather
Piel

Lingerie
Lencería

Money
Dinero

Necklace
Collar

Record/CD
Disco

Ring
Sortija, anillo

Secondhand objects
Objetos usados/de segunda
mano

Shirt
Camisa

Shoes
Zapatos

Silver
Plata

Skirt
Falda

Socks
Calcetines

Suit
Vestido

Tie
Corbata

Toy
Juguete

Trousers
Pantalón

Watch
Reloj

Wool
Lana

TIME

Half an hour
Media hora

Quarter of an hour
Cuarto de hora

It's midnight
Es medianoche

It's noon
Es mediodia

It's one o'clock
Es la una

NUMBERS

1 uno
2 dos
3 tres
4 cuatro
5 cinco
6 seis
7 siete
8 ocho
9 nueve
10 diez
11 once
12 doce
13 trece
14 catorce
15 quince
16 dieciseis
17 diecisiete
18 dieciocho
19 diecinueve
20 veinte
21 veintiuno
22 veintidos
30 treinta
40 cuarenta
50 cincuenta
60 sesenta
70 setenta
80 ochenta
90 noventa
100 cien
1,000 mil
2,000 dosmil
5,000 cincomil
1,000,000 un millon

first
primero/a

second
segundo/a

third
tercero/a

fourth
cuarto/a

fifth
quinto/a

Conversion tables for clothes shopping

Women's sizes

Shirts/dresses

UK	USA	EUROPE
8	6	36
10	8	38
12	10	40
14	12	42
16	14	44
18	16	46

Sweaters

UK	USA	EUROPE
8	6	44
10	8	46
12	10	48
14	12	50
16	14	52

Shoes

UK	USA	EUROPE
3	5	36
4	6	37
5	7	38
6	8	39
7	9	40
8	10	41

Men's sizes

Shirts

UK	USA	EUROPE
14	14	36
$14^{1}/_{2}$	$14^{1}/_{2}$	37
15	15	38
$15^{1}/_{2}$	$15^{1}/_{2}$	39
16	16	41
$16^{1}/_{2}$	$16^{1}/_{2}$	42
17	17	43
$17^{1}/_{2}$	$17^{1}/_{2}$	44
18	18	46

Suits

UK	USA	EUROPE
36	36	46
38	38	48
40	40	50
42	42	52
44	44	54
46	46	56

Shoes

UK	USA	EUROPE
6	8	39
7	9	40
8	10	41
9	10.5	42
10	11	43
11	12	44
12	13	45

More useful conversions

1 centimetre	0.39 inches	1 inch	2.54 centimetres
1 metre	1.09 yards	1 yard	0.91 metres
1 kilometre	0.62 miles	1 mile	1. 61 kilometres
1 litre	1.76 pints	1 pint	0.57 litres
1 gram	0.035 ounces	1 ounce	28.35 grams
1 kilogram	2.2 pounds	1 pound	0.45 kilograms

A   B   C

Where to shop

Nightlife

1

Estación de Santa Justa

C. P. Picasso

Car. de Carmona

Calle Arroyo

Capuchinos   Calle María Auxiliadora

C. José Laguillo

C. Juan Ant. Cavestany

Ronda

Calle

del

Calle   Recaredo

Aven.

Calle

2

C. S. J. de Rivera

Calle Muñoz León

PZA CORDOBA

Murallas

Convento de Santa Paula

PZA PONCE DE LEÓN

Casa de Pilato

C. Alhóndiga

San   Luis

Calle   de

C. Arrayán

C. Castellar

Iglesia de San Luis

Iglesia San Pedro

PZA CRISTO DE BURGOS

Resolana

Calle

Feria

Calle Feria

PZA DE LA ENCARNACIÓN

PZA DEL SALVADOR

Calle

ALAMEDA DE HÉRCULES

C. Amor de Dios

PZA SAN ANDRÉS

Pal. Lebrija

C. Cuna

Calle las Sierpes

C. Jesús

PZA DUQUE DE LA VICTORIA

PLAZA NUEVA

3

Monasterio de San Clemente

del Gran Poder

Calle Santa Ana

Convento de Santa Clara

Baños

San Eloy

C. Canalejas

PZA DE LA MAGDALENA

PTE DE LA BARQUETA

Nueva

C. Alfonso XII

Guadalquivir

(Canal de Alfonso XIII)

Torneo

Calle

Museo de Bellas Artes

Calle Marqués de Paradas

Arjo

Camino

de

los

PZA DE ARMAS

Calle

Estación autobuses

4

C. Albert Einstein

Descubrimientos

La Cartuja

Monasterio de Santa María de las Cuevas

PTE DE CHAPINA

Carretera a Huelva (N 341)

Calle

Calle   América   Vespucio

Calle Inca Garcilaso

A   B   C

with coffee and *churros* in the early hours. There's good reason for this nocturnal exuberance – the sun, which shines endlessly, can sometimes burn the city out and plunge it into a lethargy that takes a while to wear off.

treasures, Seville is equally impressive and majestic by day – the cathedral, Giralda, Alcazar, Archivo de Indias, there's any number of symbols of the city's glorious past, a blend of the Moorish conquest, the age of discovery and the Golden Age. If you thrill to the mention of names such as Murillo, Velázquez, Valdés Leal and Zurbarán, then Seville is right up your street. There's scarcely a building – church, convent, museum, even administrative building – that does not house a work by at least one of these legendary artists, who have all enriched the Andalucian capital in their own style.

it all. Nor have the gourmets been forgotten – you can feast on Serrano ham, sherry and olive oil, as well as superlative pastries and other gastronomic vices – endless temptations, which even though prepared by nuns, are impossible to resist. If you thought that Seville was the beautiful sleepy-head of Andalucia, suppressed by religion and fettered by tradition, you'll be surprised to find a modern city, dynamic, vibrant, and rich in culture, with its eyes firmly fixed on the future.

If the feverish activity of Seville's nightlife leaves you any spare energy – and if you do things the Andalucian way and take the obligatory siesta between 2 and 5pm, that shouldn't be a problem – take a look around the city. From the tiny paved streets of the San Vicente district through the wide green spaces of the Parque de María Luisa, along the Guadalquivir river, taking in the Macarena district, home of the zealous worshippers of La Macarena, or onto Cartuja island, where Expo '92 was held – the city is inviting and romantic wherever you stroll. When it comes to unveiling its

If you've had your fill of culture, zip off to the buzzing Triana district, haunt of most of the city's artisans. The ceramics, tiles and traditional embroidery are all they're cracked up to be. To pass yourself off as a local, pop in to Lina's and get measured up for a bullfighter's suit of lights or try a *mantilla* carelessly thrown over your shoulders with a fan for the ultimate in cool. If you yearn for high street boutiques stocked with haute couture or classic, timeless fashion, Seville has

How to get to Seville

In summer the midday heat is suffocating and the locals flee the centre of town, heading for the coast in an all-out assault on the nearest resorts. Life only gets back to normal in September. Autumn is when most of the rain falls, though the levels rarely break any records.

The best time to pay a visit to Seville is in the spring.

THE IDEAL TIME TO VISIT

In spring the jacaranda trees which border Seville's streets are in flower, the mottled bougainvilleas bloom in the courtyards of the houses and the little wrought iron balconies are adorned with a thousand varieties of plants. The temperature is pleasant – between 16 and 30°C (61 and 86°F), just right for visiting monuments or museums and just as good for meandering about or having dinner al fresco. Spring is also the time when the great festivals kick off. April and May are especially important for Easter Week and the Feria. The only downside is that accommodation needs to be booked in advance.

GETTING THERE

BY PLANE

The easiest way to travel to Seville for a weekend from the UK or Ireland is by air – it's the quickest and generally the most economical option. Flights from London take approximately two and a half hours. British Airways flies daily (except Saturday) to Seville from Gatwick and Iberia operates direct daily flights from Heathrow. Those travelling from Ireland will have to travel via London and travellers from the USA, Canada, Australia and New Zealand will have to change or stop over en route in a European city such as

London, Frankfurt, Paris, Madrid or Barcelona. Check with your local travel agent for flight details and options or try looking on the Internet. Another, albeit less practical, option is to fly to Madrid and take the AVE (high-speed) train to Seville.

FROM AUSTRALIA AND NEW ZEALAND

There are no direct flights to Seville from Australia and New Zealand, but it is possible to stop over in other European cities, such as London, en route. Check with your travel agent for flight details or try looking on the web.

BY TRAIN

From continental Europe, the train is an option for those going to Seville for more than a couple of days, since it may require a night on board. The train journey from the UK can take up to 30 hours.

Trains from European countries to Spain terminate in Madrid or Barcelona and are run by **Iberail** from France, Italy, Austria and Switzerland. The national train network, known as **RENFE**, is very extensive, with services tailored to all budgets. The high-speed AVE train (*Tren de Alta Velocidad Espanola*) links Seville, Cordoba and Madrid and is extremely efficient if relatively expensive. The fare includes a money-back guarantee should the train arrive at its destination more than five minutes late. It provides a 2 hour 30 minute connection from Madrid to Seville every hour. The journey from Barcelona to Seville takes nine hours.

The train journey from the UK or Ireland takes up to 30 hours in total. You can cross the English Channel by ferry or take the Eurostar (☎ 08705 186 186, www.eurostar.com) to Paris and from there board the *Francisco de Goya Trenhotel* (hotel train). This is an overnight service with sleeper accommodation that leaves

AL ANDALUS EXPRESO

If you fancy seeing Andalucia in style, treat yourself to a seat on board the Al Andalus Expreso, a luxury Belle Epoque 'hotel on wheels' and Spain's own version of the Orient Express. It pulls 14 original carriages, all built between 1900–30, and travels at a leisurely pace around Seville, Cordoba, Jerez, Granada and Ronda, departing either from Seville or Madrid between March and November. For more information check the Rail Europe website: www.raileurope.com

Paris daily at around 8pm and arrives in Madrid at approximately 9am the following morning. Eurodomino and Interrail cards are valid on these journeys, subject to the usual conditions.

Santa Justa railway station is one of Andalucia's latest landmarks. It is spacious and user-friendly, with a large self-service café, gift shops, newsstands, cashpoint machines, money-changing facilities and a left-luggage office. It is located only about five minutes from the city centre by car or bus (10–15 minutes on foot), and there's a large taxi rank at the front.

BY COACH

Travelling by coach to Seville for a weekend is not really an option due to the length of the journey, but you might consider coach travel for a longer stay. **Eurolines** have departures from London Victoria coach station on Monday and Saturday at 7.30am, with arrival in Seville at 6.15pm on Tuesday and Sunday respectively. For more information call ☎ 08705 143 219 or try their website: www.eurolines.co.uk

Seville's main coach station is located in the centre of town at Plaza de Armas (☎ 954 908 040). It's a modern building with several ticket windows, an information desk and a shopping mall. The **Alsa** coach company operates routes to destinations throughout Spain from here.

USEFUL WEBSITES

www.lastminute.com
www.expedia.co.uk
www.travelprice.com
www.ebookers.com
www.sispain.org
www.accommodationonline.co.uk

TOUR OPERATORS

You might like to compare prices from some of the UK tour operators that organise weekend breaks:

BUDGET

Over the last few years prices have soared in Spain – and Andalucia is no exception. Gone are the days of bargain hotels and huge meals for a few pesetas. As well as general rises in the cost of food and accommodation, the differences between high, mid- and low season prices have got much greater throughout the region, making cheap summer breaks a thing of the past.

Bridge Travel Services
55-59 High Road, Broxbourne
Herts. EN10 7DT
☎ 0870 727 5973
✆ 01992 456 609
email:
cities@bridgetravel.co.uk

Lupus Travel
Triumph House
189 Regent Street
London W1B 4JS
☎ 020 7306 3000
✆ 020 7287 2142
email:
admin@lupustravel.com

Kirker Holidays
New Concordia Wharf
Mill Street, London SE1 2BB
☎ 020 7231 3333
✆ 020 7231 4771
email:
cities@kirker.itsnet.co.uk
www.kirkerholidays.com

FROM THE AIRPORT TO THE CITY CENTRE

San Pablo de Sevilla airport lies 7 km (4.3 miles) north of the town on the road between Madrid and Cádiz.

☎ 954 510 677/
954 672 981/
954 449 000

There are a number of different options for getting to the city centre.

BY AIRPORT BUS
The **Amarillos Tour** buses run every half-hour from the airport to the city centre terminus at Puerta de Jerez. They run from 6.15am until 11pm and cost around €2.

BY TAXI
In Seville the taxis are comfortable and quicker than the bus. Taxis waiting at the airport can take you anywhere in the city (there are however some restrictions – pedestrian zones and other roads that are inaccessible to cars). A 10–15 minute ride to the city centre will cost around €20.

Radio-Taxi de Sevilla
Av. Kansas City, 42
☎ 954 580 000

CONSULATES IN SEVILLE

Australian Consulate
Federico Rubio, 14
41004 Seville
☎ 954 220 971
✆ 954 211 145

British Consulate
Plaza Nueva, 8B
41001 Seville
☎ 954 228 875
✆ 954 210 323

Canadian Consulate
Avenida de los Pinos, 34
41927 Mairena del Aljarafe
(Seville)
☎/✆ 954 768 828

US Consulate
Paseo de la Delicias,
41012 Seville
☎ 954 231 885
✆ 954 232 040

GETTING USED TO THE EURO

Since 1 January 2002 the euro has replaced the official currency of 12 European nations, including Spain. The peseta ceased to be legal tender on 28 February 2002. The euro, which is divided into 100 cents, has a fixed exchange rate of 166.386 pesetas. There are plenty of cash machines in the city and you can withdraw cash easily using a credit card. If you need to carry large sums of money around with you, it's wise to take traveller's cheques.

In Seville prices shoot up during the major fiestas and accommodation is at a premium during *Semana Santa* (Holy Week) and during the Feria. In general, spring and autumn are classed as mid-season, while summer is priced as low season due to the heat and the fact that everyone wants to get out of the cities and be near the beach.

Dinner in a good restaurant will cost between €18–24, while a snack in a tapas bar will range from €6–9. A cup of coffee is about €1 and a soft drink €0.75. A short taxi ride costs around €2, a cinema ticket €5, while a seat for a flamenco performance or a play will range between €9 and €21.

On the other hand, entry to public museums is free to citizens of the European Community although entry charges apply to monuments and other sights (see p. 33).

FORMALITIES

EU-citizens only require an identity card or passport. Citizens of the USA, Canada, Australia and New Zealand don't require a visa, just a passport. Foreign embassies are all located in Madrid.

CUSTOMS

In June 1999 duty-free allowances were abolished between EU countries, therefore EU citizens can take up to 800 cigarettes, 90 litres of wine and 10 litres of spirits when leaving Spain. If you enter Spain from a non-EU country, however, you can only take with you 200 cigarettes, 2 litres of wine, 1 litre of spirits and 60cl of perfume duty-free.

HEALTH AND INSURANCE

No vaccinations are needed for travel in Spain. EU citizens are entitled to basic health care in case of illness or accident. Make sure you obtain an E111 form (available from UK post offices), to enable you to recover any medical expenses you may incur on your trip.

Casa de Socorro
(Health Centre)
Calle Menendez Pelayo
☎ 954 411 712

Hospital Universitario Virgen del Rocío
Av. Manuel Siurot
☎ 955 012 000/954 248 181

Medical emergencies
☎ 061

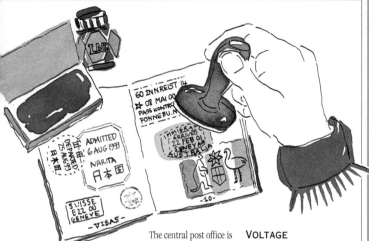

There's just one number for the **fire brigade**, the **police** and the **Civil Guard**: ☎ 112.

It's important to take out comprehensive travel insurance to cover theft, as pickpockets are not unknown and thieves are amazingly efficient. Paying for your trip by credit card may cover you for some medical assistance and lost luggage, so check with your credit card company before you leave.

LOCAL TIME

Spain is one hour ahead of GMT, except from the end of March to the end of September, when the difference is 2 hours. To sample the true Andalucian lifestyle, you really need to adjust to the times of meals. Lunch is usually between 1.30 and 2pm, and dinner is eaten very late, at 10pm. Shops are generally shut between 2 and 4pm, and banks and museums are generally open all day (until 7 or 8pm), although some close between 2 and 4pm.

The central post office is open from 8am to 10pm and bars and clubs don't really begin to buzz until around 1am, so serious clubbers will need a good lie-in to prepare for the long night ahead.

VOLTAGE

The electric current in Spain is 220 volts, as in most of the rest of Europe. The plugs have two round pins so make sure you take an adaptor if you want to use any equipment.

USEFUL ADDRESSES AND INFORMATION

SPANISH TOURIST OFFICES WORLDWIDE

UK & Ireland
22-23 Manchester Square
London W1M 5AP
☎ 020 7486 8077
𝔽 020 7486 8034
email: londres@tourspain.es

Australia and New Zealand
c/o Spanish Tour Promotions
178 Collins Street
Melbourne
☎ 03 9650 737

USA
666, 5th Avenue, 35th floor
New York NY 10103
☎ 212 265 8822
www.okspain.org

8383 Wilshire Blvd
Beverly Hills
Los Angeles CA 90211
☎ 213 658 7188

845 North Michigan Avenue
Chicago IL 60611
☎ 312 642 1992
1221 Brickell Avenue
Suite 1850
Miami FL 33131
☎ 305 358 1992

WEBSITES

There are some good websites with plenty of tourist information. Try:
www.tourspain.es
www.okspain.org
www.sispain.org
www.andalucia.com
www.sevilla5.com

SEVILLE'S RELIGIOUS TRADITIONS

It's often said that Spain is one of the European countries where religious sentiment and practice remain most active, which is very true. Lesser-known, however, is the extent to which these feelings are so powerfully expressed in Andalucia. In Seville, a devout city teeming with churches, the year is regularly punctuated by any number of religious occasions. In spring, Catholic fervour reaches its zenith, spilling out onto the streets during the *Semana Santa* (Holy Week).

there is plenty here to satisfy the devotional thirst.

A PROFUSION OF RELIGIOUS BUILDINGS

There are 70 churches in Seville, each claiming to be the city's biggest or most beautiful. And that doesn't take into account the monasteries, convents or tiny chapels that can be found down every street. The arrival of the Moors, followed by the advent of Catholicism, resulted in a combination of styles that has contributed hugely to the city's architectural splendour. If all roads – for pilgrims, that is – do not lead to Seville, then at the very least

RELIGIOUS CONFRATERNITIES

The majority of practising Catholics in the city are grouped together by district or by family into one of 57 organisations of religious affiliation known as *cofradías*. The loyalty of these groups is focused on a local favourite statue depicting Christ or the Virgin. This creates an unexpected competitive edge during the processions of Holy Week (*Semana Santa*).

Which icon will be judged the most beautiful – the Virgen de la Macarena (see p. 52) or the Virgen de Triana (see p. 61)? Which statue will be the most inspiring – the Jesús del Gran Poder (see p. 57) or El Cachorro de Triana (see p. 60)?

THE PROCESSIONS

Holy Week (the week before Easter) commemorates the Passion of Christ and his resurrection. Each community takes its own Via Dolorosa to the cathedral as an act of penitence. Statues of Christ or the Virgin are paraded through the city on *pasos*, huge platforms that weigh between 1,500 and 2,000 kg (3,300–4,410 lbs). Up to 50 men carry them on their shoulders and their slow march makes the long robes of the statues swing in time with the solemn music. The most impressive processions set off at daybreak

HOLY WEEK TRADITIONS

• Women wear a *mantilla* (lace veil) decorated with carnations on Holy Thursday but without decoration on Good Friday, as a sign of mourning.

• The traditional fare for Easter Week is *torrijas* (bread soaked in milk and fried) and *pestiños* (delicious sweets, dripping with honey).

on Good Friday, when the Esperanza de Triana, Jesús del Gran Poder and the celebrated Virgin of la Macarena make their appearances (see p. 54).

SAETAS

The sound of dark and doleful singing can often be heard as the processions meander past. These are *saetas*, sung a capella by the women and completely improvised. These piercing cries are gypsy in origin and express compassion for the death of Christ. Whenever a *saeta* gets under way, the *pasos* grind to a halt and silence falls, impressive in its respect and gravity.

EASTER WEEK, A SPECIAL AMBIANCE

Time seems suddenly to stand still. The heady smell of incense, the stern-faced crowds

in mourning, the ponderous processions and the sombre music recall an earlier age. As night falls, the city's penitents, lit only by candlelight, have a rather disconcerting appearance. Their long robes and tall pointed hoods render only their eyes visible and give them an intimidating look. And when the masses begin to let loose the full fervour of their emotions, it's not a spectacle for the faint-hearted.

THE EL ROCÍO PILGRIMAGE

Not far from Seville, in the Huelva mountains, huge crowds from Andalucia and, indeed, from all over Europe gather at Whitsun for another procession. In a convivial atmosphere, pilgrims make their way on foot, on

horseback or in carts to the shrine of the *Blanca Paloma* (the white dove) as the Virgen del Rocío (Virgin of the Dew) is known. It's the largest and most famous of all the pilgrimages in Spain. However, the carefree nature of the procession leaves you ill-prepared for the emotional scenes of religious fervour that take place afterwards.

TAPAS – AN INTRICATE ART

Did you know that the word *tapa* means 'cover'? Originally, it seems that tapas were simply pieces of sausage or chorizo that were placed on top of a glass of wine to stop the flies dropping in. Over time, tapas became more and more elaborate and nowadays they are intricately composed delicacies to be enjoyed casually while strolling with friends from bar to bar. Tapas are part and parcel of the festive and relaxed atmosphere you cannot fail to feel part of.

A SHORT HISTORY OF TAPAS

According to legend, it was King Alfonso X 'the Wise', who ordered all the inns in Castile to serve a little snack with every glass of wine, though whether this was purely for pleasure or for reasons of hygiene is unknown. Another version has it that the custom originated much later, in the 19th century, with a waiter who used to cover glasses with a slice of sausage to stop sand being blown into the wine.

Alfonso X

TAPAS, FROM *TORTILLA* TO *PAELLA*

The pace of modern life has led to the ubiquitous rise of fast food. Instead of a midday meal, the Sevillian locals now prefer tapas, which were previously no more than a little something designed to keep you going until dinner. Tapas used to consist mostly of olives, slices of meat or *tortilla* (Spanish omelette). Nowadays, these elements still prevail but more elaborate combinations are also brought into play and even established staples of Spanish cuisine such as *paella* can be served up as tapas.

THE CHEF'S SUGGESTIONS

When it comes to tapas, bravery is normally rewarded. Let yourself be tempted, try absolutely everything, and don't restrict yourself to just the best known varieties! *Cabrillas:* small, highly flavoured snails.

Flamenquines: deep-fried rolls of meat stuffed with ham.

Papas aliñás: potatoes spiced up with a sauce of onions, peppers and tomatoes.

Papas alioli: potatoes in a heady garlic sauce.

Cazoletitas: small individual portions of stew.

Pescaíto frito: mouth watering pieces of fried fish.

Pringás: bite-size toasted sandwiches filled with chorizo, sausage and bacon.

With Friends or Not at All

There's little point waiting to be invited round to your friends' homes in Seville. The glorious weather that blesses Seville most of the year makes most people meet up outside rather than at home. Propped up at a bar, small groups while away the time, snacking on

tapas washed down with a glass of wine or beer. After a few laughs and general banter the conversation more often than not returns to the subject of food.

Some Pointers if You Want to *IR DE TAPEO*

You'll certainly want to blend in with the crowd, so here are a few golden rules to get the most from your bar-hop:

• the best fun is had in small groups of four to six people;

• tapas appreciation is a relaxed, refined art that has to be acquired … standing at the bar;

• eat little but diversify – try different bars;

• indulge in *cuchareo*: everyone tastes everyone else's tapas;

• don't forget to buy your round, *una ronda*. You'll be demonstrating your *convidá*, or fellowship;

• above all, leave your worries at home and enjoy the atmosphere. This is not the time to bother with serious issues. If you want to start an argument, it should only be about who has chosen the best tapas.

SEVILLE AND ITS PAINTERS

Amongst all the arts that are so well represented in the ancient city of Hispalis, the one that is truly Sevillian is painting. It can be admired not just in the museums but throughout the city – unexpected treasures are to be found in many historic or religious buildings and monuments. During the 16th and

Zurbarán, Saint Hugo in the Refectory

17th centuries the Seville school of painters produced vast quantities of pictures to beautify their city.

of Europe set up studios in Seville where they could share knowledge and skills. Some of these Flemish painters were quick to swap their names for something more local sounding: Pedro de Campaña (1503–63), who painted the *Descent from the Cross* in Seville's cathedral, was originally known as Peter Kempeneer. We should also mention Alejo Fernández (1475–1546), who was the real founder of the first Sevillian school and whose name you'll certainly see adorning many a canvas.

HISTORY AT A GLANCE

The rich outpouring of art in Seville during the 16th and 17th centuries is closely tied to its history. The 16th century was the age of discovery and exploration in the New World (see pp. 30–31) that led to great prosperity. The commercial monopoly that Seville gained on the European stage at this time made it a metropolis of boundless wealth – the population expanded, religious

buildings proliferated and art, sustained by a flourishing economy, underwent a renaissance.

PAINTERS OF SEVILLE ... FROM NORTHERN EUROPE

In fact, the cultural renaissance in Seville was galvanised by the arrival of a posse of architects, sculptors and other European painters in search of fame and fortune. Many artists from the north

Fernández, The Virgin of the Sailors

Murillo

THE SECOND SCHOOL: PAINTERS FROM SEVILLE

The Golden Age of Sevillian painting really started in the 17th century. In this period, some really great names

latter two artists are the most important contributors to this Golden Age of Sevillian painting and many examples of their work survive in a number of the city's religious buildings.

JUAN DE VALDÉS LEAL

Valdés Leal's particularly tormented personality pervades his work in such a way that it never fails to have an effect on his audience, and with good reason. His masterworks depicting death are doubtless the most dramatic in the whole history of art. His varied

MURILLO'S PRIVATE KINGDOM

Bartolomé Esteban Murillo is *the* Sevillian painter. His reputation in Seville's artistic circle was such that he is now fêted in every part of the city. Both his name and his art can be seen everywhere, there's a monument to him in the most prominent position in front of the Museo de Bellas Artes (see p. 56) and the Barrio de Santa Cruz has become his personal domain. He is buried under Plaza Santa Cruz where the *Cruz de la Cerrajería*, a 17th-century sculpture by Sebastián Conde is also displayed. The house where he spent his final years is on Calle Santa Teresa (see p. 41) and nearby, the wonderful gardens that border the district are named after him (see p. 40).

Valdés Leal, The Flagellation of St Jerome

began to emerge. Francisco de Zurbarán (1598–1664) was a genuine Andalucian who often worked in Seville, notably completing a commission for the Convent de la Merced. Diego Velázquez (1599–1660), a native of the city, left Seville in 1623 to become official painter at the Spanish court. Juan de Valdés Leal (1662–95) settled permanently in 1658 and Bartolomé Murillo (1617–82) never abandoned the city of his birth. These

Murillo, The Immaculate Conception with God the Father

and copious output is imbued with a baroque darkness, and his fear of death can be clearly seen in the paintings that are displayed in the cathedral (see p. 36) and in the Hospital de la Caridad (see p. 47). The latter contains the famous 'Vanities': *Finis Gloriae Mundi* (The End of Worldly Glory) and *In Ictu Oculi* (In the Blink of an Eye), very characteristic examples of his macabre style. His son and assistant, Lucas (1661–1725) is considered one of the very best of Seville's fresco painters.

TORO, TORO!

The *corrida* or bullfight, is a festival of colour – the *albero* (white) of the sand, the *traje de luces* (suit of lights) of the bullfighter, the scarlet of the *muleta*, the fuchsia pink of the capes and the white and yellow paint of the arena. In dazzling light beneath the sun's scorching heat, the highly charged atmosphere is almost palpable. Sevillians, bound by tradition, put aside their differences for this overwhelming obsession. The *toro* (bull) and the *torero* (bullfighter) are quintessentially Andalucian.

EL PASEILLO, THE GRAND OPENING

The spectacle begins with a colourful procession, known as *el paseillo*. To the sounds of *paso dobles* played by the stadium band, all the participants line up before the presidential box. The *toreros* and their *quadrilla* (a small team of banderilleros and picadors) dressed like old style pages, are led on by the *alguaciles* on horseback. The *toreros* wear an embroidered silk cloak and a hat. If you watch carefully, you'll see them draw the sign of the cross in the sand with their feet to commend themselves to God.

IT'S A MAN'S WORLD

It's the job of the *mozo de estoques*, the matador's valet, to dress the bullfighter in a ceremony that is exclusively reserved for men. Only the very nearest and dearest are allowed access to the room in the Melia Colón Hotel (see p. 66) where the careful preparations are made. Once they have arrived at the arena, the bullfighters gather in the tiny chapel of La Maestranza before the event starts to ask the Virgin for her protection. The matadors' mothers and wives often prefer to give the bullfight a miss and instead spend the long hours of waiting in diligent prayer.

LA PUERTA DEL PRÍNCIPE

It's through this gate, on the west side of the arena, that the very best *toreros* leave the ring, hoisted onto the shoulders of their adoring fans (see p. 46). To enjoy this privilege, they will have had to follow some strict rules and carried off the spoils of the fight. To be carried out of the Puerta del Príncipe in this triumphant way is the dream of every *torero*, especially if the triumph coincides with the Feria.

NOT FORGETTING THE BULLS

The success of a bullfight depends as much on the bravery of the bull as on the courage of the *torero*. The six bulls in each event are supplied by the same breeder, some of whom, such as Miura or Dolores Aguirre, have acquired mythical status in the bullfighting world. Bulls lacking in fighting spirit are sent back to their pen to the accompaniment of whistles from the crowd. On the other hand, the president can choose to reprieve a bull after an exceptional fight.

A CONTROVERSIAL ENCOUNTER

Three *toreros* take part in each bullfight. Easily recognised by their fabulous gold-embroidered *trajes de luces* (suits of lights), their assistants wear suits with black or silver embroidery. According to ancient tradition, each *torero* must fight two bulls – the most senior *torero* going first. As the fight ensues, the interplay of costumes and *banderillas* (spiked sticks) creates a brightly coloured ballet in the arena, before the *torero* is left to face the bull alone. He swaps his cloak for a *muleta* (small cape) and a word … and so the fatal endgame begins.

word – he waves different coloured handkerchiefs to indicate whether a bull should be finished off or given a reprieve. At the end of each fight, everyone stands to applaud not only the *torero* but the bull as well. If you're in any doubt, just keep an eye on your neighbours. If you follow their lead, you won't go too far wrong.

EL AFICIONADO, A KNOWLEDGEABLE AND PASSIONATE AUDIENCE

You won't have any trouble distinguishing the crowd's approving 'Olé!' from their discontented whistling. The president alone has the final

A Moorish heritage

Seville's past is bound to a thousand-year heritage that has only recently begun to be acknowledged as a crucial aspect of Andalucian culture. You may not notice the traces of Seville's Arabic past which are dotted here and there, but you will be immersed in an atmosphere, a city and a way of life that owes much, if not all, to centuries of Islamic occupation and integration.

CENTURIES OF ARAB OCCUPATION

The year 712 marked the beginning of the Moorish occupation of Seville. Subsequent dynasties of Arabs, known as Moors, Almoravides (Berber tribes) and then Almohades in the 12th century left their mark on present day Andalucian culture. The Catholic reconquest, launched in the 13th century and not completed until the end of the 15th century, happily failed to eradicate all traces of this exceptional Arabic heritage.

MOORISH ARCHITECTURE

A number of Seville's buildings bear witness to the continuing presence of Moorish art in Andalucia – the Torre del Oro (see p. 46), the Palacio de Pedro I in the Alcázar (see p. 39), certain parts of the Casa de Pilatos (see p. 43), and some 13th-century churches, not to mention the elegant minaret known as La Giralda (see p. 36). The quintessentially Spanish fusion of Arabic and Western styles is known as Mudéjar art. Meaning 'he who has been given leave to remain', the word was applied to captured Muslims who were subsequently authorised to stay in their home area after the Christian reconquest. This magnificent hybrid style continued to be popular until the 18th century and was at its zenith in the 16th century when Alfonso X and Pedro I employed the talents of Mudéjar craftsmen to build their churches and palaces.

Don Pedro I

MOORISH GARDENS

Seville owes its love affair with nature and landscaped gardens to its Moorish rulers. Following Arabic tradition, the gardens of Seville are peaceful and spacious, oases of calm for contemplation ... or secret assignations. It is noticeable that all these gardens are designed around a refreshing pool. Some even have irrigation channels or small waterfalls, while colourful ceramic tiles (*azulejos*) also play an indispensable part in

the enchantment of the scene. Water plays with light, light plays with colour, and colour plays with fragrance – the gardens of the Real Alcázar (see p. 39), awash with their striking bougainvilleas, should not be missed.

THE ANDALUCIAN HOUSE AND ITS HAVEN, THE 'PATIO'

In true Arabic style, Andalucian houses are protected from the gaze of outsiders. Their entrances onto the street are barred by a *cancela* (wrought iron grille), which separates the entrance from the inner courtyard. Wrought iron

covered windows set into the whitewashed walls allow those inside to see out without being seen. The Moorish-style 'patio' at the heart of the house serves as an open-air lounge. In the centre of this courtyard garden lies a fountain, surrounded by

masses of sweet smelling plants – geraniums, jasmine and orange trees – set against a background of colourful, decorative tiles. For the best examples of these verdant courtyard gardens head for the Barrio de Santa Cruz district (especially Callejón del Agua). There's an annual 'prettiest patio in Seville' competition which takes place in May.

AZULEJOS

The Spanish word for tile, *azueljo*, comes from the Arabic word *azulayj*, meaning 'little stone'. The techniques for making these enamelled ceramic squares were developed by the Moors. They can be found all over the city, on the façades of public buildings or decorating houses. The culmination of this art is the creation of sophisticated mosaics with highly stylised geometric or organic decorative motifs in

FROM MINARETS TO BELL-TOWERS

La Giralda (1184) closely resembles the minarets of Rabat (Hassan's Tower) and Marrakesh (the Kutubia), from the tops of which the call of the muezzins rings out across the city. This former minaret of the Great Mosque has considerably influenced elements of Sevillian architecture and was the forerunner of other similar towers decorated in Islamic style – for example, the tower of the church of San Marcos (see p. 54) which dates from the 14th century, or that of San Pedro.

beautiful, rich colours. If you want to see tile craftsmen at work, try Seville's Triana district (see pp. 58–61).

FESTIVALS AND TRADITIONS

Whenever it's time for one of Seville's colourful festivals, the city's pulse quickens. Spring is particularly festive as it kicks in with the famous 'Feria de Abril', which takes place over the two weeks following Easter. Sevillian and Andalucian folklore has forged a strong identity at the forefront of the country's popular arts. Flamenco music and dancing can be experienced throughout the city, and the locals need only the most feeble excuse to sport picturesque costumes with vibrant colour schemes.

THE *FERIA DE ABRIL*
The Real de la Feria, a 7-hectare (17-acre) park, like a city within a city in the south of the Los Remedios district, hosts a week long 24-hour festival party. The April Fair is one of the greatest festivals in the world and marks the arrival of spring and the start of the bullfighting season.

ORIGINS
In 1847, the authorities were instructed by Isabella II to organise a great money making venture in the shape of an annual market (*Feria*). It was from this livestock market that an unparalleled festival was born. The success of the first event was such that the market's bullfighting festival became a worldwide attraction, known as the *Feria de las ferias*, the queen of fairs. Nowadays, the livestock fair, which began it all, is just an attractive sideshow with the shepherds and the breeders being judged in marquees.

Isabella II

The market was moved in 1973 and now takes place in Los Remedios.

A FESTIVAL FOR THE WHOLE TOWN
The livestock fair is only of interest to professionals today. Much more fun is the donkey and horse 'Pirate fair' which is held on the Cadiz road. Even though the Feria has evolved considerably over the last thirty years, it's still the town's most symbolic festival. It's a 24-hour affair – by day fantastic floats and extravagantly costumed women, dressed to the nines in their flounced dresses and *mantillas*, parade through the streets for the *cabalgata*. By early evening, everyone has trooped off to the Maestranza bullring to see the matadors in action and after dark, the pulsating rhythms of flamenco music fills the night air with a series of concerts and shows. As dawn breaks, *caldito de*

puchero, a thick stew, is the favoured breakfast, followed by a visit to the Patio des Gitans, a *caseta* where the best flamenco dancers perform, further accompanied, of course, by hot chocolate and some *churros*.

WHERE TO FIND FLAMENCO

Those keen to have a go themselves can try La Carbonería, Calle Levíes, 18 (see p. 117). Other flamenco evenings take place at El Arenal, Calle Rodo, 7 (€28, see p. 116), at La Casa Anselma, Pagés del Corro, at Los Gallos, Plaza de Santa Cruz (€22, see p. 115), at El Patio Sevillán, Paseo de Colón, 11 (€25), and at El Palacio Andaluz, Av. Auxiliadora, 18 B (€24).

CASETAS

Casetas are little entertainment booths, made from scaffolding and covered with green and white drapes. Sevillians come here to meet up with friends, watch flamenco dancing or singing and enjoy a couple of glasses of *manzanilla* sherry. Locally made food is also available. The *casetas* are usually rented out by the local authorities to various associations, *confradías* (religious groups), or even individuals. It's not the easiest thing in the world for a tourist to get invited along, but some local societies and organisations open their *casetas* to the public. Be warned however, that the addresses can change from one year to the next, so it's a good idea to check the Feria maps which are available from the Tourist Office at Calle Arjona, 28 (☎ 954 505 667, 🄵 954 505 672, turismo@sevilla.org).

CUSTOMS AND TRADITIONS

The traditional women's dress is known as *traje de flamenca* or *traje de gitana* and not, as it is sometimes called, *traje de faralaes*. The costume is derived from the everyday dress of 18th-century Spanish women, although it is highly adaptable to the fashion of the day. The only rule is that it should never be worn with a *cordobès* hat. For their part, the men dress in the *campo* style — boots, trousers tied round the waist with a red sash, white shirt and short

jacket. On the subject of drinking, don't forget that *manzanilla* sherry should never really be mixed with *fino* and that drinking *rebujito* (San Lucar *manzanilla* sherry mixed with a type of lemonade) is currently all the rage.

GETTING TO THE FERIA

A special bus service leaves from the Prado de San Sebastián, taking you right to the main entrance of the park for around €1. Alternatively, you can use the circular bus routes, C1 and C2 or route 14. A taxi will set you back around €3 and it's about €4 to park a car for the day. If you really want to go to town, you can buy a traditional outfit and blow €60 by rolling up in a magnificent carriage or even on horseback.

THE HORSEBACK PARADE

In the mornings, the streets of the Real de la Feria are given over to the *paseo de caballos* (horseback parade), each rider with a beautiful Sevillian lady riding pillion. Formerly, the

CALENDAR OF FESTIVALS AND HOLIDAYS

Festivals
- April: *Semana Santa*
- April–May: Feria (Spring Fair)
- Itálica: international dance festival (May)
- Bienal de Arte Flamenco: last two weeks in September (even years)
- International jazz festival (early November)

Public holidays
1 January: New Year
6 January: Epiphany (Reyes)*
28 February: Andalucia Day
19 March: San José*
1 May: Labour Day
30 May: San Fernando
25 July: Santiago*
15 August: Assumption
12 October: Spanish National Holiday (Christopher Columbus Day)
1 November: All Saints' Day
6 December: Day of the Constitution
8 December: Immaculate Conception
25 December: Christmas Day

* Can be replaced by the Autonomous Communities with another date.

cavaliers sought to impress families who were looking to marry off their daughters and even to this day horses remain central to the festivities. A 'Spanish'-trained horse, which arches its neck and lifts its forelegs high, is a sure sign of a certain social standing.

FLAMENCO

Flamenco is sung, hummed and played in all the city's smoky bars as well as on the streets of its numerous districts. Not many Sevillian children

say the word derives from the Arabic term *felaomengu* (peasant in flight), which would suggest that the gypsies are of Moorish descent. A third variant has it that the word derives from the Hebrew *cante jondo* sung in synagogues (*jom tode* signifying 'festival day'). In fact, the combination of singing, dancing and guitar strumming represents a hybrid of Arabic, Jewish and gypsy cultures that found its present form back in the 18th century.

play truant from their flamenco classes. They don't require much invitation before they're clacking their castanets or banging their tambourines on their dancing shoes.

THE ORIGINS OF FLAMENCO

The origins of flamenco are somewhat vague. Even the meaning of the word is

ambiguous. Dictionaries suggest that *flamenquería* (gallantry) refers to Flemish singers employed at the court of Carlos V who were known as *flamencos*. Alternatively, some

PASSION AND EMOTION

Flamenco songs are renowned for expressing pain and the suffering felt by the 'travelling community'. They also symbolise both the misery and

joy of life, encompassing the full gamut of human emotions. Following the example of jazz, flamenco music lends itself well to improvisation, and spontaneous interpretation

can be intense and vibrant. The *cante flamenco* also includes dances such as *alegrías*, *bulerías* or *sevillanas* that are highly popular at festival time.

THE LANGUAGE OF FLAMENCO

Partly invented by gypsies, flamenco language isn't easily grasped at first hearing. It employs typical expressions of gypsy origin, such as *bari*, *cani*, *calorro* or *cale*, all meaning 'gypsy'. In the gypsy family, the mother is the *matu*, the father the *patu* and the son is the *chorreles*. Any non-gypsy is a *payo* or a *gacho* and his wife is a *gachi*. A specialised dialect is also used to describe the different ways of interpreting a flamenco song; for example, a *palo seco* means an unaccompanied song. The power and mystery of these impenetrable songs relies on the enigmatic *duende*, a word almost impossible to translate, which describes the beguiling frisson that the performer communicates to his audience.

HANDICRAFTS OF SEVILLE

Ceramics are undoubtedly the most common traditional form of craft, and the reputation of Seville's workshops, which has been widespread for centuries, is still formidable, especially those of the Barrio de Triana. But the artisans' skill is also applied to other crafts. Seville's passion for festivals and traditional rites has led to great skill in the creation of fabulous accessories, such as embroidery, fans, shawls, combs and castanets.

TILES AND CERAMICS

Sevillian ceramics first made their appearance in the 12th century thanks to Arab

decorative skills. Several manufacturers take the styles of 14th and 15th century Islamic–Spanish studios as their inspiration. Today, ceramics seem to be experiencing a boom. Every design and style is available, from everyday ceramics for use in the home to unique

pieces of designer art. Workshops can mostly be found in the Triana district in boutiques or studios (see pp. 96–97). The walls and floors of many houses are covered in mosaics made from Sevillian *azulejos*, which have enjoyed

a huge reputation since the Middle Ages. The most opulent Mudéjar decoration is the incomparable *cuerda seca* tile, with its metallic sheen.

EMBROIDERY

The traditions of textile manufacture have been handed down by generations of women who were brought up from a tender age to embroider, mastering a variety of skills over the centuries. Embroidery has since become something of a luxury product. Hand-made articles such as tablecloths, napkins, curtains, bed linen and cushions inevitably form the mainstay of any young Sevillian couple's wedding list. This craft requires a high degree of skill as well as an extensive knowledge of sewing and embroidery techniques specific to the region (see p. 107).

TRADITIONAL ACCESSORIES

The finely carved tortoiseshell combs and embroidered shawls are almost irresistible

(see pp. 108–109). These pretty accessories are indispensable for the traditional *flamenca* look ... if you know how to wear them. Sevillians will tell you that to carry the look off, you need a certain level of grace combined with a touch of artistry. The shawl, which is slipped over the shoulders and the arms, should be worn as casually as possible. The combs, which fix the lace *mantilla* to the hair, are traditionally worn elegantly high on the head.

FANS...

Contrary to what you may be led to believe, the fan was not entirely a Spanish invention. It actually first appeared in Asia in the Middle Ages and didn't reach Spain until the 16th century. The court of the kings of France was especially taken with the accessory in the 18th century. Seville is currently the guardian of the fan's timeless appeal, one always being conveniently located in a handbag for use on hot summer days. The most expensive fans are made of carved wood and are painted by hand.

... AND CASTANETS

Castanets or *castañuelas* are yet another seductive element in the array of the *flamenca's* accessories. The elegance and spirit of this percussion instrument accompanies traditional Spanish dances and some Flamenco songs. Castanets are made of two round carved pieces of wood, (in rare cases, ivory) and are concave like chestnut shells. The two pieces are tied together with a length of string. If you get the chance, see if you can make them work – you'll soon see how fiendishly difficult it can be.

(see pp. 108–109).

KEEP A LOOK OUT FOR...

Bordado español
A type of embroidery made up of an infinite number of repeated patterns, forming a decorative border around the edge of a piece of cloth.

Bordado de Lagartera
One of the most popular forms of embroidery. Its geometric or floral designs are very simple and delicate.

Encaje de Malla
A type of lace, made from embroidered thread, which originated from the area around Puebla de Guzman (Huelva). It is highly valued for its wonderfully complex designs.

Bordado de Navalcan
These designs are always geometrical and are used to edge pieces of linen.

ANDALUCIAN CUISINE

Everything conspires to make Andalucian cooking special. The high quality local produce has been enriched over the centuries by exposure to foreign cultural influences. The Andalucians are proud of their gastronomic history and careful to preserve its quality. At

the Taberna del Alabardero (see pp. 72 and 105), Seville's Hotel School helps to maintain standards and improve the delicious Andalucian cuisine even further.

THE MEDITERRANEAN DIET

The Mediterranean diet followed in the southern countries of Europe is recognised by experts to be one of the healthiest. If that's what you're looking forward to in Seville, you'll already know that vegetables, fruit and grilled fish are a better choice than the fried food, cheeses and meat selections which are featured here. You should bear in mind, however, that Spain is the world's second largest consumer of fish after Japan and that one of the key ingredients of Sevillian cooking, olive oil, is considered to be one of the principal features of a balanced diet.

CHACINERÍA

This word describes the various meats (*jamón*, *cerdo*, *chorizo* – ham, pork, sausage) that come from the Andalucian

mountains. The charcuterie from the Sierra de la Huelva, where they breed the highly prized Iberian pig, is well known for its superior quality and it was in Huelva that the term '*Jabugo*' was originally coined. The best variety of *jamón Serrano* (smoked ham) is the *jamón de pata negra*, taken from pigs that

are fed exclusively on mast (acorns). It's best eaten in very thin slices.

PESCAÍTO FRITO AND OTHER FISHY DISHES

You won't find this crispy delight prepared in this way anywhere else. The fish, which are especially chosen for their small size, are rolled in flour and fried in olive oil. *Pescaíto frito* should always be accompanied by a glass of *manzanilla* or *fino* sherry. You'll also find it hard to resist *tortillitas de camarón*, small omelettes stuffed with tiny shrimps.

by some good coffee. You can find all these and more at Viña & Olivo (Cruces 7, ☎ 954 422 078, open every day, 11am-2pm, 5-9pm).

OLIVE OIL

Olive oil is Mediterranean cooking's great ambassador. Nutritionists can't praise its virtues enough. There are dozens of varieties of this golden liquid, each with its own particular use – *ojiblanco* is perfect for salads, *arquebino* gives mayonnaise an especially sweet taste and the stronger-tasting *picual* is perfect for sprinkling on some toast with a little salt, making an ideal breakfast when accompanied

WINE

The wide-ranging diversity of Spanish wine is matched by its increasingly remarkable quality. But as we're in Seville, we'll concentrate on Andalucian wines. The most prestigious are still the Jerez sherries from Cadiz. They come in a variety of types: the *finos*, which are dry and clear, the *manzanillas* from Sanlúcar de Barrameda, the *amontillados*, rather smoother, and the *olorosos*, with their fortified alcohol content.

In Cordoba, the Montilla-Morilès wines have an identical range. You can also enjoy the liqueur-like wines and *olorosos* from Málaga. Among the most famous brands to look out for are La Ina from Domecq or Tio Pepe, from the cellars (*bodegas*) of González Byass. As for *manzanillas*, try the *Solear* from the Bodega Barbadillo.

LIVING LIFE TO THE FULL, ANDALUCIAN STYLE

Naturally, Sevillians love to stroll about their city, taking advantage of the wonderful weather and the outside living it offers. They also have a great weakness for spending all hours of the day and night chatting in bars. You too will learn to appreciate the coolness of the long evenings and to catch up on missed sleep during the *siesta* when the unforgiving sun beats down outside.

A GOOD START TO THE DAY

Some of the traditions that Sevillians enjoy have taken on the status of a full ritual. As an outdoor life and endless conversation are the norm, what better way to begin the day than to stroll to the bar on the corner for a chinwag over the morning's news? Propped up against the bar, you can order *churros* (long, ridged doughnuts), or *tostados* (toast), preferably sprinkled with olive oil, washed down with a *café con leche* (coffee with hot milk), or a *cortado* (espresso with milk). For a more extravagant choice, try *chocolate con churros* (hot chocolate with *churros*).

SIESTA FIESTA

The custom of taking a siesta is popular in hot countries and little understood elsewhere. In a city like Seville, however, where the temperatures in summer can regularly soar over 40°C (104°F) in the shade, the siesta is an essential part of life. Although it's understandable that some tourists want to make the most of their time in the city, the rest of the population can easily be forgiven for having a lie-down after lunch. Sleeping isn't strictly obligatory but

nevertheless, between 2 and 5pm, the city falls into a deep lethargy and everything shuts down. It doesn't come back to life again until early evening when a cool breeze starts to blow the cobwebs away.

A SAIL DOWN THE STREETS

During the summer, the Sevillian sun – the sun of doom as they call it here – becomes public enemy number one. In the streets, pedestrians hug the walls in a search of shelter. Shade

El APERITIVO

Be warned! Unlike some other countries, the custom of taking an aperitif, which is well-established in Spain, is not something just confined to the early evening. The Sevillians' convivial spirit prompts them to meet up for a tipple any time after 1pm. Before heading home for lunch, they like to retire to a favourite, well-frequented spot, to meet up with friends. This custom is particularly well observed at weekends. All it takes is some *fino*, a few olives and good company.

...comes a luxury commodity, which explains why the city centre's narrow streets are covered with enormous white veils that stretch between the buildings on either side – and naturally, corporate business is unable to resist such a perfect opportunity for a little publicity.

'PATIOS' AND COURTYARD GARDENS

Long before the sails were installed, Sevillians found another way of escaping the sun. 'Patios' were a Roman innovation adopted by the Arabs. Filled with potted plants and flowers and built around a central fountain, they are cool havens of tranquillity. In Moorish times, these courtyard gardens provided separate meeting places for men and women. The gentle trickling of the fountains once enabled people to talk without being overheard, but now the sound simply serves to refresh

the mind and the body. As you stroll along the streets of the city centre, you can glimpse some of these charming patios and gardens hidden away behind semi-closed doors. Most are not open to the public but the Casa de

Pilatos (see p. 43) and the Palacio de Lebrija (see p. 44) both have charming courtyards that you can visit.

GIVE ME AIR!

Sevillians have famously adopted a number of stratagems to combat the heat. There's one that you can even take home with you – the fan. Everywhere you go, in churches, cafés, buses, you'll see women vigorously fanning themselves. Compact and practical, fans come in a vast range of shapes, colours and sizes, plain, intricate or ornamented and mostly made from wood or plastic. Some examples, made from ivory or mother-of-pearl and often

hand painted, are collector's items. There's a specialist shop, Rubio, which

stocks a huge selection of beautiful fans, which make ideal gifts. It's well worth a visit (Sierpes, 56, ☎ 954 226 872).

1492-1992 – SEVILLE, CAPITAL OF EUROPE

Seville's present splendour is not exclusively down to the contribution of Moorish culture. This Andalucian city owes its physical features equally to the conquest of the New World: the great explorers found in Seville a confident partner to act as a depository for this new wealth. The confrontation between old and new continents galvanised the emergence of a new, cosmopolitan city, alert to the whole world.

García Ibanez, Christopher Columbus received by the Catholic kings

TREASURES OF THE NEW WORLD

The great discoveries made by the explorers were for the most part prompted by a need to find a new route for the spice trade. They may not have expected to bring back such unknown riches, but over the course of the centuries, potatoes, maize, coffee and chocolate, to name but a few, profoundly transformed

THE GREAT EXPLORERS IN SEVILLE

The Catholic monarchy of Spain was the only kingdom to unconditionally sponsor the great explorations of the 15th and 16th centuries. Situated on the Guadalquivir river, opening onto the Atlantic, Seville was ideally positioned for the commerce between Andalucia's fertile lands and

New World wealth. In 1493, Christopher Columbus chose to embark on his fourth voyage from Seville. For his first circumnavigation of the globe, Magellan set off from Triana, sailing down the Guadalquivir to Sanlúcar to reach the Atlantic. Amerigo Vespucci was also an adopted son of Seville and spent many years in the city working for a merchant.

The Columbus monument in the Jardines de Murillo

Magellan

European diet. Better still, in the Americas the Europeans discovered gold and silver mines. These precious metals were kept as ingots before being melted down to be struck as coins in Seville's Casa de la Moneda.

GRANDEUR...

Seville quickly established a trade monopoly between the Old and the New World. The city alone was responsible for chartering the 'armadas' which set out for the colonies and for welcoming them back again. The galleons and light, manoeuvrable

Christopher Columbus

caravels were highly efficient at transporting tons of commercial produce from the Americas. The foundation of the Casa de Contratación

(Chamber of Commerce) in 1503 allowed Seville to control the trade far more efficiently and attracted a vast cosmopolitan society made up of bankers, traders, and artists from the whole of Europe, all of whom contributed to the city's economic and cultural renaissance.

... AND DECLINE

From the second half of the 17th century, Seville experienced an economic

Christopher Columbus' caravel

decline from which she never recovered. The rest of Spain, embroiled in political problems, dragged the city and its bright future down with it. The Guadalquivir, Seville's vital river, which had been responsible for so much of the city's great expansion, now contributed a considerable factor to its downfall – its channel silted up, compromising its ability to take commercial traffic. In 1717, the Casa de Contratación was relocated to Cadiz, which became a symbolic end to Seville's Golden Age.

ARCHIVO DE INDIAS

Initially built to house the *lonja* (Trade Exchange), this building was later redesignated by Carlos III as the 'Indies Record Office'. Today, these archives provide one of the major sources for the study of American history. Countless maps and documents demonstrate step by step how the states of South America were first colonised ... and then decolonised in their turn (see p. 38)

Carlos III

EXPO '92

The theme of the 1992 World Expo, held in Seville, was the 'age of discovery'. The five hundred year anniversary of the New World's discovery could not have chosen a better host. Just as the period of colonisation had led to great opportunities for modernisation and expansion, Expo '92 gave Seville an international reputation, which contributed to the economic regeneration of the city and the region. It also led to the building of the AVE, the Spanish high speed train, an airport and many new highways – allowing Seville to unveil its wealth of riches to the world.

What to see Practicalities

GETTING ABOUT

BUSES

Because it has no metro, Seville has a comprehensive bus system that covers the centre of town as well as the main places of interest. It's run by the Transportes Urbanos de Sevilla (TUSSAM) company, whose buses are easily recognisable in their orange livery. Thankfully, in summer they are all air-conditioned. The *circulares* are just the job for people staying in the old town. The four different routes, numbered from C1 through to C4, take you round the city centre or down by the Guadalquivir river. These 'circular' routes are complemented by a network that covers the entire city.

Information and tickets can both be found at the main stations, la Barqueta and Prado San Sebastián, and information and route-maps are available from: Plaza Nueva, Plaza de la Encarnación, Archivo de Indias, Macarena, Puerta Osario, Gran Plaza, and Pasarela-Prado.

The first buses depart at 6am from Monday to Saturday and 7am on Sundays and public holidays. Night owls need to know that the last buses depart at 11.30pm in winter and 12.30am in summer, followed by a special night bus service that comes to a halt at 2am.

If you're not planning to use the bus very often, it is possible to buy a single ticket (€1) from the driver, but you must have the correct change. For regular users, *Bonobus* vouchers are a very practical way of getting about the system and give the best value for money – the book of ten vouchers works out at half the price of single tickets. Furthermore, there's no limit as to where you can go and they have no expiry date. They cost €4.50 and are available from tobacconists and newspaper kiosks, or from the TUSSAM ticket offices at the route terminuses. Here they can also provide you with a *carta para turistas*, a tourist bus pass, which lasts for three days and can be used up to five times in one day. They cost €6.50, or there's a seven-day version for €10.

TUSSAM

General information:
☎ 900 710 171
TUSSAM Office
Calle Diego de Riaño, 2
☎ 954 557 201
www.tussam.es

TOURS OF THE CITY

The 'Sevirama City Tour' is a double-decker bus trip that gives you a bird's eye view of Seville's principal tourist attractions. It departs every half hour from 10am until 11pm from the Torre del Oro or the Plaza de España. You can stop off at any one of four places: Torre del Oro, Plaza de España, Isla Mágica and Monasterio de la Cartuja. Tickets cost €9 for adults and €5 for children under 12. If you're lucky and keep your eyes peeled, you might be able to find a 'Sevirama City Tour' pamphlet in one of the tourist offices which offers a reduction on the ticket prices if you show it to the driver.

Sevirama City Tour
Paseo de Colón,
next to the Torre del Oro
☎ 954 560 693
📠 954 560 365

BY CAR

Cars are banned from the city centre and it's nearly impossible to find anywhere to park. Theft is also a major problem. As for the traffic, most drivers seem to ignore the road-signs or rights of way. You should therefore take great care if you do decide to drive. Most travellers who prefer individual transport take a taxi, which is a lot less bother, and safer, than a hire car.

BY TAXI

Taxis in Seville are white with a yellow stripe down the side and a logo on the rear doors. They are good value for money, even at night when the tariff goes up slightly. You can pick one up almost anywhere; if their little green light is on it means they are free.

Radio Taxi de Sevilla
Av. Kansas City, 42
☎ 954 580 000

Tele-Taxi
Av. de la Paz, 63
☎ 954 622 222

Radio Teléfono Giralda
Av. Innovación, edif.
Convención 201
☎ 954 675 555

ON TWO WHEELS

You can always hire a motorbike or a scooter, but keep a careful lookout for other drivers … the rules of the road aren't exactly adhered to.

Moto Rent
Calle Padre Mendez
Casariego, 19
☎ 954 417 500
📠 954 425 506

Hiring a 125cc machine will cost about €30 per day or €60 for three days. A scooter costs around €21 per day.

HORSE-DRAWN CARRIAGES

A ride in a horse-drawn carriage through the streets of Seville might seem a little old hat but it is nevertheless an excellent way of getting to see the city. A 45-minute ride should cost about €25. If your Spanish isn't up to haggling, try to seek out a

young driver who is more likely to speak English. Carriages leave from the cathedral, María Luisa park or near the Torre del Oro (Paseo de Colón).

IN A BOAT OR A PEDALO

This is an outing with a difference. Take to the river for a relaxing trip, with the Torre del Oro and the Plaza de Toros as a backdrop. To hire a boat try:

Barco Lola
Paseo de Marqués de Contadero
☎ 908 155 151

Cruceros del Sur
Paseo de Colón, 11
☎ 954 561 672

Buque El Patio
Paseo de Colón, 11
☎ 954 213 836

POST

It costs €0.42 to send a
postcard or letter to anywhere
in Europe. You can buy
stamps (*sello*) from
tobacconists, newspaper
kiosks and stationery/book
shops. The yellow letterboxes
are easily recognisable and
the larger post offices are
generally open Monday to
Friday 8am-9pm, Saturday
9am-1pm.

Main Post Office
Av. de la Constitución, 32
(opposite the cathedral)
☎ 902 197 197
Open Mon.-Fri., 8.30am-
8.30pm, Sat. to 2pm.

PUBLIC TELEPHONES

Seville's telephone network is
managed by Telefónica. Try to
avoid phoning from your
hotel as the charges are
exorbitant. It's much better to
buy a phone card, which can
be used in a phone box,
though sometimes you have
to dial a code number.
They're on sale in kiosks or
tobacconists in values of €6,
€12 or €30. The phones also
take coins (minimum €0.15).

For international calls, dial
00 + the country code. From
the UK, dial 00 34 followed by
the Andalucian number.

Telephone Exchange
Plaza de la Gavidia, 2

**National directory
enquiries**
☎ 003

**International directory
enquiries**
☎ 025

INTERNET CAFÉS

Internet centres can be found
dotted all over the city. You
can pay by the hour or a
one-off fee and surf the net or
email to your heart's content.

Workcenter
Calle San Fernando, 1
(opposite the university)
☎ 954 212 074
24-hour info line:
☎ 902 115 011

Office services, stationery, photocopying and Internet access, open 24 hours a day. €0.75 for the first ten minutes, cheaper thereafter.

Seville Internet Center
Calle Almirantazgo, 2 (1st floor)
☎ 954 500 275
✆ 954 500 520
www.sevillecenter.com
Open Mon.-Fri. 9am-10pm, Sun. noon-10pm.

TOURIST OFFICES

The city's Tourist Offices give out information on sites of interest, museums, trips, emergency services and accommodation. You'll also find details of festivals in the area. Local newspapers and city guides are another source of information on times and places. A large, detailed map of the city and the surrounding area costs €0.60, while others – not quite as comprehensive – are free of charge. You can also ask for a guide to the local transport systems, with a map of stations and routes. The offices are open Monday to Friday 9am-7pm, and Saturday and Sunday until 2pm.

Oficina centro
Av. de la Constitución, 21
☎ 954 221 404
Open Mon.-Fri. 9am-7pm, Sat. 10am-2pm.

Costurero de la Reina
(see p. 49)
Puerto Delicias, 9
☎ 954 234 465

Oficina Municipal de Turismo
Calle Arjona, 28
☎ 954 505 600

Estación de Santa Justa
Av. Kansas City
☎ 954 537 626

GUIDED TOURS

You can ask at the central Tourist Office about the various agencies offering guided tours. The following are the most reliable:

Passion Tours
Calle Rivero, 9

☎ 954 563 245
✆ 954 500 815
passiontours@teleline.es

Guidetur
Calle Mateos Gago, 29 (ground floor)
☎ 954 227 324 or 954 222 374
guidetur@esbasa.com
This organisation provides guides for individuals and groups and offers various tours lasting a day or half a day (from around €120).

A.P.I.T.
Av. de la Constitución, 9
☎ 954 210 037
✆ 954 228 337
apitsevilla@alehop.com

Monumental
Calle Real, 27
☎/✆ 954 761 280
monumental@softhome.net

Around the Cathedral, seville's historic centre

The cathedral district is never anything but lively, thronging with visitors from every corner of the globe. The most impressive buildings in the city are located here, between the Puerta de Jerez and the cathedral, a monumental Gothic masterpiece which sits majestically next to the sublime Mudéjar palace, the Alcazar. Beauty and history combine to give a fantastic first impression of Sevillian culture.

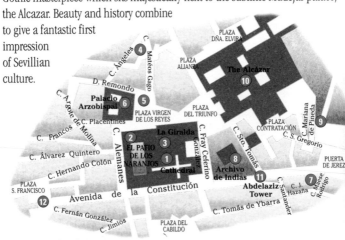

❶ The Cathedral★★★★
Plaza Virgen de los Reyes
☎ 954 214 971
or 954 563 321
❺ 954 564 743
Open Mon.-Sat. 11am-5pm, Sun. 2-6pm (these times are subject to change). Entry charge except on Sundays.

Following the expulsion of the Moors in 1248, the Great Mosque was rededicated as a Christian cathedral and was used as such for 150 years. In 1401 the by now rather dilapidated mosque was demolished, leaving only its minaret – the Giralda, and work began on a new building. Completed in 1506, this magnificent edifice is the third biggest cathedral in the world, after St Peter's in Rome and St Paul's in London, and has been declared a world heritage site by UNESCO. Its five naves and 25 chapels boast many wonderful works of art and fabulous treasures, including the tomb of Columbus (1891) and a huge altarpiece, which is a magnet for visitors. (See p. 122.)

❷ La Giralda★★★
On the same site as the cathedral.

The emblematic and monumental Giralda tower is a graceful example of Islamic architecture. It has wonderful Almohad-style ornamentation and if you're brave enough to

MAGNA HISPALENSIS, THE MEASURE OF SEVILLE

'Let us build a church so huge that those who see it will think we are fools', the Christians of Seville are said to have declared in 1401, when the Great Mosque was demolished. The dimensions of the cathedral are certainly impressive, covering more than 23,000 sq m/247,570 sq ft, with five naves, seven gates and 25 chapels. The Giralda, the old Almohad minaret, is almost 100 m (300 ft) high and contains 25 bells. Its weather vane, the *Giraldillo*, a revolving bronze statue of a pregnant woman, weighing 2 tonnes, is the biggest in the world.

stone fountain with a bowl from the Visigoth era. A building on the east side houses the Biblioteca Colombina, with its fine collection of ancient documents and books.

❹ Bar La Giralda★★
C. Matéos Gago, 1
☎ 954 227 435
Open every day 9am-midnight.

tackle the steps to the top, the view will blow you away. Once the minaret of the Great Mosque, it was converted into the cathedral's bell tower and, along with the Patio de los Naranjos, is all that remains of 12th-century Seville.

❸ El Patio de los Naranjos★★
On the same site as the cathedral.

This charming remnant of 12th-century Seville was once the courtyard of the Great Mosque. It can be reached either through the cathedral or via the Puerta del Perdón, which retains its fine bronze portals decorated with Arab characters. The orange-tree courtyard, surrounded by a series of Mudéjar arches, has a

It's worth taking a break for a beer at one of the

tables outside the Cervecería Giralda on Calle Mateos Gago just for the view of the Giralda. Built on the site of a Moorish bath, this bar is renowned for its excellent range of tapas. Try the scampi wrapped in a filet of fish with a cream and mushroom sauce. Lunch is served until 5pm if, in true Andalucian style, you're running late. The cooking is good and the prices are reasonable.

❺ Plaza de la Virgen de los Reyes★★

This square is usually filled with tourists taking a welcome rest after a long day's sightseeing. It's also the best starting point for a stroll through the tiny streets of the Barrio de Santa Cruz, or to listen to the calls of the carriage drivers tempting you, in their thick Andalucian accents, to take a tour of the Parque de María Luisa. Along one side of the square you'll find the Convento de l'Encarnación, where nuns sell 'home made' religious artefacts from behind their grille.

❻ Palacio Arzobispal★★

Plaza Virgen de los Reyes
☎ 954 227 163
Visits by appointment.

Located on the left side of the square, opposite the Giralda, it's hard to miss this superb example of a Sevillian baroque façade. Built around two courtyard gardens, one with a fountain crowned with a marble statue of Neptune, this Episcopal palace was completed by Manuel Arias in 1717. It houses a collection of pictures, including examples by Zurbarán and Murillo, as well as an archive of priceless documents dating from the 12th century.

❼ Mama Goye★

C. Maese Rodrigo, 8
☎ 954 501 571
Open every day 11am-11pm.

This ice cream parlour, which overlooks the Avenida de la Constitución, offers visitors a chance to cool off with a delicious Argentinian ice cream. It's well worth a

detour, so take a refreshing pause and sample the huge variety of stunning flavours on offer before you tackle the exhausting climb to the top of the tower of the Giralda – especially in summer.

❽ Archivo de Indias★★

Av. de la Constitución, 3
☎ 954 225 158
or 954 500 528
Open Mon.-Fri. 10am-1pm.
Free entry.

This huge Renaissance-style building, which used to be the Casa Lonja (the old Exchange), has been a

repository for the historical archives since 1785. Today it contains displays of archive material about the Spanish conquests and colonisation of the New World together with numerous maps and drawings dating from the end of the 15th century to the 19th century. Most of the documents remain in storage due to their fragile nature, but those on display give visitors a fascinating insight into the administration of Spain's former American colonies.

❾ Sevilla Mágica★★★

C. Mariana de Pineda, 11
☎ 954 563 838
Open Mon.-Fri. 10am-9pm,
Sat. 10am-8pm, Sun. 10am-1pm.

bags, T-shirts, fans, ceramic figurines, ashtrays, picture-frames and jewellery. You just won't know where to begin!

10 The Alcázar★★★★

Patio de Banderas
☎ 954 502 323
www.patronato-
alcazarsevilla.es
Open Tues.-Sat. 9.30am-
7pm, Sun. 9.30am-5pm.
Entry charge.

waterfalls. The sole remaining Almohad-style building in the Alcázar is the Patio del Yeso (plasterwork courtyard), which dates from the end of the 12th century. (See p. 127.)

11 Abdelaziz Tower★

The small hexagonal tower on the corner of Calle Santo Tomas and the Avenida de la Constitución is an original Islamic building dating from 1180. According to some historians, it once contained

a flag given by King Fernando III to a group of Scottish soldiers, in gratitude for their assistance. They were accorded the privilege of running the flag up the tower when the first Christian troops entered Seville in the Reconquest.

12 CELIS ARTESIANA

Plaza de San Francisco, 14
☎/📠 954 224 829
Open Mon.-Sat. 11am-
8.30pm, Sun. 11am-3pm.

A must for all bullfighting aficionados, this shop displays a selection of traditional costumes, with all the accessories, along with a fine collection of old posters, most to do with the Feria. You'll find souvenirs and gifts, all emblazoned with the shadow of a bull, as well as postcards, though these, at €0.60, are dearer than most. Glamour doesn't come cheap!

The visitors' entrance to the Seville Alcázar, or, to give it its correct name, the Reales Alcázares, is through the Puerta del León, which is surmounted by glazed tiles showing a coat of arms with heraldic lions. Prepare to journey through several centuries of history during your visit to this palatial complex, which is a mix of Islamic and Christian styles and influences. It's the oldest royal residence in Europe and is sumptuously decorated. Wander through the luscious greenery of its gardens, which are dotted with grottoes, pavilions, resplendent fountains and

This pretty boutique has a huge selection of souvenirs for your perusal. They are typically Sevillian and quite tasteful. You can buy huge posters advertising the spring festivals, silk embroidered shawls, antique *azulejos*, striking neckties, leather

The Barrio de Santa Cruz
Smells and colours of Seville

On the left bank of the river lies the former Jewish quarter of Santa Cruz, with its tiny paved streets, little flower-lined squares, scented orange trees, shady courtyards and whitewashed walls. The delightful atmosphere is the essence of

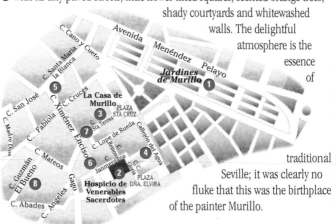

C. Cano y Cueto
Avenida
Menéndez
Pelayo
C. Santa María la Blanca
Jardines de Murillo ❶
❺
C. San José
C. Cruces
C. Fabiola
C. Ximénez Enciso
La Casa de Murillo ❸
PLAZA STA CRUZ
PLAZA Sta. Teresa
❼
C. Lope de Rueda
Callejón del Agua
C. Madre Dios
C. Mateos Gago
C. Reinoso
❻
Janmeralnga
❹
C. Guzmán El Bueno
❽
C. Abades
C. Angeles
❷
Gloria
Hospicio de Venerables Sacerdotes
PLAZA DÑA. ELVIRA

traditional Seville; it was clearly no fluke that this was the birthplace of the painter Murillo.

❶ Jardines de Murillo★★

Free entry through a number of gates (Plaza Alfaro, Plaza Refinadores, Plaza Don Juan de Austria).

As you wander among the bougainvilleas, palms and jasmine in these lovely gardens, fill your lungs with the intoxicating scent of the orange-blossom. You can

almost feel the spirit of Murillo in the air. He's not the only famous character celebrated here. There's also a monument to Columbus with a detailed model of the *Santa María* – the ship in which he sailed to the 'Indies'.

❷ Hospicio de Venerables Sacerdotes★★★

Plaza de los Venerables, 8
☎ 954 562 696
Open every day 10am-2pm, 4-8pm.
Guided tours in Spanish. Entry charge.

The Hospicio de Venerables Sacerdotes was built to care for old and infirm priests. Its frescoes, by Juan de Valdés Leal, are particularly fine and a Sevillian-style courtyard leads to a spectacularly ornate

church with an astonishing *trompe l'oeil* ceiling. It's an exceptional example of Sevillian baroque architecture.

❹ El Corral de Agua★★★★

Callejón del Agua, 6
☎ 954 224 841
(booking line)
❻ 954 561 204
www.andalunet.com/corral-agua
Open Mon.-Sat. 1-4pm, 9pm-midnight.

This is the perfect place to stop and try gazpacho, sole in orange or a crème caramel.

3 LA CASA DE MURILLO
C. Santa Teresa, 8
Open Mon.-Fri. 10am-1.30pm, 4-6.30pm.
Free entry.

Only the ground floor of Murillo's house is open to the public: It boasts an interesting collection of documents which detail the history of Sevillian painting in Murillo's time. There are a number of rooms set round a very pleasant courtyard, each displaying old engravings and pictures showing scenes of religious and daily life.

he tranquil setting is the erfect spot for a well-deserved reak. Some of the tables in e lush courtyard are set out round a fountain and the enuine Andalucian cooking delicious.

5 Plaza Santa María la Blanca★★
This was once a meeting place for semi-free black slaves during the Golden Age and is now a place where tourists relax at numerous outdoor cafés. Opposite, on the Calle

Santa María la Blanca, you'll find a former synagogue, now converted into a baroque-style church. There never was a better time to get over any aversion to all things baroque – it contains paintings by Murillo and an altarpiece by Luis de Vargas depicting the *Pieta*.

6 Coco Sevilla★★★
C. Ximénez de Enciso, 2
☎ 954 214 532
Open every day 10.30am-8.30pm.

This superbly decorated art and craft shop is run by four artists specialising in different fields. Tiles, fans and ceramics have been remodelled into works of art and brought bang up to date with modern designs.

Prices are reasonable considering that many of the pieces are high quality one-offs. You'll fall head over heels in love with the stunning painted silk shawls with their contemporary motifs.

7 Las Teresas★★
C. Santa Teresa, 2
☎ 954 213 069
Open Mon.-Fri. 9am-4pm, 6pm-midnight, Sat. and Sun. 11am-4pm, 8pm-midnight.

This atmospheric café-bar with its bullfighting-oriented décor was once an old grocery store and is an ideal spot for a swift glass of wine or for some tapas out on the terrace. On the menu are old family recipes using a fine variety of meats, cheeses and Serrano ham from Huelva and Salamanca.

8 Galeria Haurie★
C. Guzman el Bueno, 9
☎ 954 225 726
F 954 563 233
Open Mon.-Fri. 11am-2pm, 6-9pm, Sat. 11am-2pm.

Each month this gallery has a themed exhibition by a different artist. If you're passing through this back-street with its superb traditional houses, stop and take a look at the paintings and figurative sculptures by a variety of local, Andalucian and Spanish artists.

El Centro, heart of sevillian life

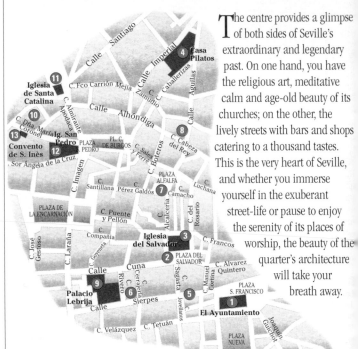

The centre provides a glimpse of both sides of Seville's extraordinary and legendary past. On one hand, you have the religious art, meditative calm and age-old beauty of its churches; on the other, the lively streets with bars and shops catering to a thousand tastes. This is the very heart of Seville, and whether you immerse yourself in the exuberant street-life or pause to enjoy the serenity of its places of worship, the beauty of the quarter's architecture will take your breath away.

❶ El Ayuntamiento★★★

Plaza Nueva
☎ 954 590 101
Open Tues.-Thurs.
3.30-4.30pm,
Sat. 11.30am-12.30pm.
Closed 15 July-15 Sept.
Entry charge.

You can't help but be impressed by this resplendent Renaissance building, which now houses the city hall. Its remarkable entrance gate is decorated with the figure of Hercules, the mythical founder of the city. Nearby Julius Caesar, protector and builder of the city walls sits on his throne. Inside, the council meeting chamber has a superb ornate ceiling as well as busts of the kings of Spain. (See p. 128.)

❷ Plaza del Salvador★★

The square is dominated by two monumental churches (El Salvador and San Juan de Dios) which stand on either side. When the fine weather

DOÑA MARÍA
FERNANDEZ
CORONEL

This noble lady was the
wife of Don Juan de la
Cerda, who was was killed
by King Pedro I 'the Cruel'.
When the latter decided to
marry the beautiful widow
himself, she is said to have
thrown herself into boiling
oil to disfigure herself in
order to repulse him. Left
to mourn her true love
unmolested, she founded
the Santa Inès convent
(see p. 45) where, once a
year, her remains are put
on display.

arrives, Sevillians flock to the square between 1.30 and 2.30pm for their aperitif (see p. 29). For this particular ritual they stand round upturned barrels instead of sitting at tables. You can always join them in a chilled *manzanilla* and if you're feeling peckish, there's a little kiosk which sells home made potato chips.

3 Iglesia del Salvador★★★
Plaza del Salvador
Open Mon.-Sat. 6.30-9pm,
Sun. 10.30am-2pm, 7-9pm.

This lavish baroque church is almost on a par with Seville's cathedral. It's a bit over the top, to put it mildly. It was built in 1671 on the site of an old mosque that was destroyed by an earthquake. Some traces of its Islamic past

remain, such as the orange-tree courtyard and the base of the minaret. The interior is a revelation, containing works of art by Juan Martínez Montañés, including a fine *Christ of the Passion* and the 17th-century *Crucificado del Amor*, depicting Christ on the Cross, by Juan de Mesa.

4 Casa de Pilatos★★★
Plaza de Pilatos, 1
☎ 954 225 298
Open every day 9am-7pm
(July-Sept. 9am-8pm; closed
Mon., Thur. & Sat. in Aug.).
Entry charge.

The aristocratic Medinaceli family still resides in part of this magnificent palace, with its fine combination of Renaissance and Mudéjar architecture. Here you'll find some fine earthenware, Roman statues, ornate ceilings and a superb painted ceiling by Francisco Pacheco. But if you've had your fill of art and culture, you can while away the time in the lush

greenery of the cool courtyard garden, lulled into a reverie by the gentle murmuring of the fountains. (See p. 131.)

5 Calle Sierpes★★
This street is steeped in history. It was here that Cervantes is said to have written *Don Quixote* and it once served as a trading place for medicinal plants brought back from the New World. Nowadays this picturesque street is pedestrianised and is filled with smart boutiques and fascinating craft-shops.

During siesta time it's deserted but towards evening it fills up to become *the* place to stroll and go shopping.

❻ Ochoa★
Sierpes, 45
☎ 954 228 223
❺ 954 225 528
Open every day 9am-9pm.

Ochoa is the perfect place to take a break from an exhausting afternoon's shopping. Try and drop in around tea time and you'll catch a nice cross section of cosmopolitan society. It's a very traditional café that's as good for a delicious homemade milkshake as it is for pastries, sandwiches, salads or cooked meals.

❿ El Rinconcillo★★
C. Gerona, 40
☎ 954 223 183
Open every day except Wed. 1pm-1.30am.

Founded in 1670, El Rinconcillo is Seville's oldest bar – and it looks it! This typically picturesque establishment, located just behind the Santa Catalina church, has become an institution in the area. The bar's locals and regulars have used the tiled walls to pay tribute to one of the owners, Don Agustin de Rueda Gutierrez.

❼ Plaza del Alfalfa★
Alfalfa, or 'lucerne', is a type of hay. This popular little square used to be the site of the alfalfa market. Nowadays, it's rather better suited for relaxing in the shade of its tall trees, nursing a drink. After your Sunday stroll to the pet market (see p. 100), pop into the Gran Tino bar for *café con churros.*

❽ The head of King Don Pedro★
In the Calle Rey Don Pedro, just opposite Calle Candilejo, there's a marble bust of King Don Pedro. According to legend, the king himself

ordered this bust to be made to atone for a crime he had committed. But historian Pere Florez has a different theory. His story has it that one Enrique de Trastamara killed and decapitated his own brother and displayed his head in this spot. The bust was later made to replace the grisly remains.

❾ Palacio de Lebrija★★★
C. Cuna, 8
☎ 954 218 183
❺ 954 501 029
www.palaciode lebrija.com
Open Mon.-Fri. 10.30-1pm, 5-7.30pm (4.30-7pm in winter), Sat. 10am-1pm. Entry charge.

This typical Sevillian mansion a good example of Mudéjar and Renaissance styles, house several fine collections. The huge, richly decorated rooms

re arranged around an
tractive central courtyard
arden and contain some
uperb statues and many
ther treasures. (See p. 132.)

**Iglesia de
anta Catalina**★★
Alhondiga
954 217 441
pen Mon.-Fri. 7-8pm.

a play by Cervantes Santa
atalina is depicted as a lively
eeting place for students,
o came to exchange
ighbourhood gossip which
ey would then report back
to their masters. A blind
storyteller would also draw
a crowd. Today, the sole
remnants of this colourful
local entertainment are the
bars with their open terraces
that surround the square. The
church has some interesting
elements, such as its Mudéjar
tower and fine portal.

**⑫ Iglesia
San Pedro**★★
Plaza San Pedro
☎ 954 216 858
Open Mon.-Sat. 8.30-
11.30am, 7-8.30pm,
Sun. 9.30am-12.30pm,
7-8.30pm.

Yet another church built on
the site of an old mosque.
This time, however, not
a single trace
remains of its past.
The church contains
a magnificent
altarpiece by Pedro
Delgado depicting
scenes from the
life of St Peter, as
well as *El Cristo
de Burgos* by Juan
Bautista Vazquez el
Viejo (the old), one of the
greatest exponents of Sevillian
baroque art.

**⑬ Convento
de Santa Inès**★
C. Maria Coronel
Open Mon.-Fri. 9am-1pm,
4-7pm.

Legend has it that the church
organist, Maese Perez, died
before he could play a piece
he had composed for the
Christmas Mass. Accordingly,
every Christmas night, his
haunted soul lets rip on the
organ. If this tale sends
shivers down your spine, you
can always comfort yourself
with some of the fabulous
sweets made by the convent
sisters, including the famous
Santa Inès *bollitos,* which
are only sold between October
and May.

⑭ Casa Moreno★
Gamazo, 7
☎ 954 228 315
Open Mon.-Fri. 8am-
3.30pm, 6-9.30pm,
Sat. 9am-3.30pm.

This little shop isn't much to
look at but it specialises in
Serrano ham and *queso
manchego*, a dry goat's
cheese, so you can stock up
on some of the local
delicacies. There's a bar
hidden away at the back
of the shop where some of
the locals like to hang out.

El Arenal, home of the corrida and bullfighting legends

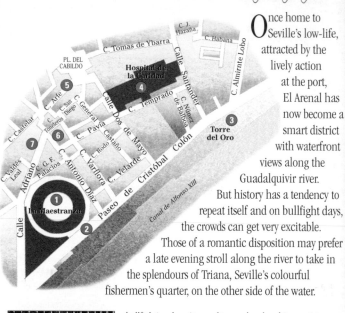

Once home to Seville's low-life, attracted by the lively action at the port, El Arenal has now become a smart district with waterfront views along the Guadalquivir river. But history has a tendency to repeat itself and on bullfight days, the crowds can get very excitable. Those of a romantic disposition may prefer a late evening stroll along the river to take in the splendours of Triana, Seville's colourful fishermen's quarter, on the other side of the water.

❶ La Maestranza★★★
Paseo de Colón, 12
☎ 954 224 577
www.realmaestranza.com
Open every day 9.30am-2pm, 3-7pm, except on bullfight days when last entry is at 3pm (excluding the chapel and the stables). Entry charge.

Seville's famous *plaza de toros* is well worth a visit, even if bullfighting doesn't appeal to you. And if you're a dedicated fan, you've no excuse for not going to a *corrida* (bullfight) and soaking up its unique atmosphere. The guided tour takes you round the ring, the museum, the medical centre, the chapel and the stables. (See p. 130.)

❷ Statue of Carmen★
Directly opposite the bullring stands a bronze statue of Carmen. Her proud, seductive look is true to her description in Mérimée's story and Bizet's opera. Bewitched by her gypsy charm, Don José abandons his promising military career and becomes a smuggler, but Carmen rejects his obsessive adoration and allows herself to be seduced by a handsome bull-fighter, a betrayal that costs her life.

❸ Torre del Oro★★★
Paseo de Colón
☎ 954 222 419
Open Tues.-Fri. 10am-2pm, Sat., Sun. and public holidays 11am-2pm. Entry charge.

The 13th-century Torre del Oro (Tower of Gold) has witnessed the city, the Triana district and the Guadalquivir rise up around it.

There's some dispute as to whether it's named after the gilded tiles that decorated its walls or the prosperous era that followed the colonization of the New World, when it was the repository for all the wealth of the 'Indies'. Once the linchpin of the Almohad city defences, it now houses a naval museum.

🅓 Hospital de la Caridad★★
C. Temprado, 3
☎ 954 223 232
Open Mon.-Sat. 9am-1.30, 3.30-6.30pm, Sun. and public holidays 9am-1pm. Entry charge.

In 1667, Miguel de Mañara founded a charity hospital for sick and destitute people wandering the streets of Seville. Built in typical Sevillian style, the hospital is accessed via two beautiful courtyards

separated by a double patio gallery. The seven panels of *azulejos* on the walls are well worth a look. The hospital's church contains some great works of art. (See p. 125.)

🅔 La Isla★★
C. Arfe, 25
☎ 954 212 631
or 954 215 376
📠 954 562 219
Open every day noon-4pm, 8pm-midnight.

If you like fresh fish, seafood and shellfish, give yourself a little treat. Occasionally it's a nice idea to forget the tapas and sit down to take time to savour some of the other delicious local specialities on offer. Located directly opposite the El Postigo craft market, this restaurant in the Calle Arfe has quality food and a warm welcome that are irresistible.

🅕 El Caballo★
C. Antonio Diaz, 7
☎ 954 218 127
Open Mon.-Fri. 9am-2pm, 5-8.30 pm, Sat. 10am-2pm.

Founded in 1892, this shop originally specialised in riding equipment. Today, it has diversified into men's and women's fashion as well as a variety of fine leather accessories.

THE IGLESIA DE SAN JORGE, THE JEWEL OF THE HOSPITAL DE LA CARIDAD★★★

This church is built in exquisite taste. It's hard not to be moved by the impressive pictures by Valdés Leal that reflect the brevity of life and the futility of worldly goods. Other superb works of art displayed here include *St Elizabeth of Hungary caring for the afflicted* and *St John of God carrying a sick man* by Murillo.

Its growing success has led to a chain of boutiques being opened throughout Spain. The branch on Calle Antonio Diaz has acres of space for fashion as well as riding gear.

🅖 Typical Spanish★
C. Adriano, 47
☎ 954 226 039
Open every day 11am-8pm.

This shop is entirely what you would expect from its name. Here, you won't be surprised to find a variety of typically Spanish gifts and souvenirs, such as bullfighting posters (you're only two minutes from the bullring) and original T-shirt designs.

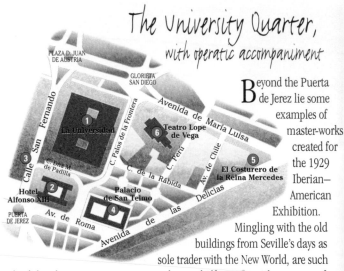

The University Quarter, with operatic accompaniment

PLAZA D. JUAN DE AUSTRIA

GLORIETA SAN DIEGO

Calle San Fernando

La Universidad ❶

C. Palos de la Frontera

Avenida de María Luisa

Teatro Lope de Vega ❻

C. Perú

Av. de Chile

El Costurero de la Reina Mercedes ❺

❸ C. Dña M de Padilla

C. de la Rábida

Hotel Alfonso XIII ❷

Palacio de San Telmo

❹

las Delicias

PUERTA DE JEREZ

Av. de Roma

Avenida de

Beyond the Puerta de Jerez lie some examples of master-works created for the 1929 Iberian–American Exhibition. Mingling with the old buildings from Seville's days as sole trader with the New World, are such splendid 20th-century monuments as the Hotel Alfonso XIII. The contrast of various architectural styles, history and legend is a feast for the eyes.

❶ La Universidad★★★★
C. San Fernando, 4
☎ 954 551 000
Open Mon.-Fri.
8am-8.30pm.
Free entry.

As you might expect from the Spanish Empire in the 16th and 17th century, the second largest building in Spain after the Escorial has no less than 44 courtyards and a stately interior that is breathtaking in its finery. Built during the reign of Carlos III, this old Fabrica Real de Tabacos (Royal Tobacco Factory) was in its time the main source of

the country's revenue and held the market monopoly until the 19th century. It now serves as Seville's University. (See p. 129.)

❷ Hotel Alfonso XIII★★★
C. San Fernando, 2
☎ 954 222 850
✆ 954 216 033
www.westin.com

The most beautiful hotel in Andalucia is a Moorish-style palace that was inaugurated by King Alfonso XIII for the 1929 Iberian–American Exhibition. A meeting-place for the wealthy and famous of the world, this haunt of the great and good of Seville boasts splendour, tradition and

hospitality. The rooms are comfortable and luxurious, with prices to match.

❸ Agua de Sevilla★★
C. San Fernando, 3
☎ 954 591 538

A new store, Agua de Sevilla, which recently opened its doors opposite the university, was the actual birthplace of

FABRICA REAL DE TABACOS

Isabel Rodriguez de Quesada, creator of the fragrances launched in 1987 that carry her name. The pretty ochre shop front conceals vast premises measuring 1,200 sq m (12,912 sq ft) and decorated in pure Sevillian style. Various elegant perfumes and jewellery are on sale in the old library as well as a range of interior design items and prêt-à-porter fashions.

4 Palacio de San Telmo★
Av. de Roma
☎ 954 597 505
Visits by appointment.

This baroque palace is named after San Telmo, the patron saint of sailors, who was priest and confessor to King Fernando III. Built in the 17th and 18th centuries,

---

'YOU'D BEST TAKE CARE...'

Did you know that Sevillian *cigarreras* (cigar girls) produced most of the cigars smoked in Europe over the past few centuries? These were the characters that gave Mérimée and Bizet the inspiration for the sensual and irrepressible femme fatale, Carmen. According to the tale, it was outside the cigar factory that Carmen and Don José, a corporal in the dragoons, first met and fell in love.

---

it was originally a nautical training centre (*Escuela de pilotos de la Carrera de Indias*). Visitors are only allowed to glimpse the exterior at present, including its fine Churrigueresque (ornate baroque) door.

5 El Costurero de la Reina Mercedes★
Paseo de las Delicias, 9
☎ 954 234 465

This little yellow and pink lodge was once the guard-house for soldiers protecting

---

members of the Royal family in residence at the Palacio de San Telmo. It became famous thanks to the charismatic daughter of the Duke of Montpensier, Mercedes, who transformed it into her own personal *salon de couture*. Although she died of consumption at a very early age, she is still remembered by the people of Seville in a song, 'María de las Mercedes'. The building is now the Seville Tourist Office.

6 Teatro Lope de Vega★★
Av. María Luisa
☎ 954 590 853/54
Box office: open 11am-2pm, 6-9pm.
☎ 954 590 867
www.andalunet.com

Seat prices at this theatre vary between about €6 and €24, depending on whether you want a box, a seat in the stalls or a view from the gods. Shows start at 9pm and include flamenco, plays and concerts. A biannual flamenco event and an international early music festival are in the pipeline.

Parque de María Luisa, a verdant retreat

Donated to the city by the Infanta María Luisa, the park was the site of the 1929 Iberian–American Exhibition. A walk or carriage ride through the gardens is a botanical journey of discovery. Giant eucalyptus, olive and palm trees bring a touch of the exotic to the heart of Seville and constructions from the 1929 Exhibition are dotted around, including the magnificent celebration of Spain's history, the 'Plaza de España'.

❶ Parque de María Luisa★★★★

Av. de las Palmeras
Open every day 8am-10pm.
Free entry.

Designed for leisure and located a stone's throw from the university, this park would be appreciated by any student. The Parque de María Luisa was originally a part of the gardens of the Palacio de San Telmo. As you stroll through the park, with its ceramic-decorated grottoes, fountains and benches, head for the Avenida de los Cisnes, which will in turn lead you down to a romantic lake. (See p. 133.)

❸ Monument to Bécquer★

By the park entrance, near the Plaza de España, stands a statue of the Sevillian poet Gustavo Adolfo Bécquer (1836–70), surrounded by three marble female figures, allegories for the ages of love: the passion of youth, serene love and forgotten love. It's a heartfelt tribute by the Sevillian sculptor, Lorenzo Coullant Valera.

❹ Museo de Artes y Costumbres Populares★★★

Plaza de América
☎ 954 232 576
🖷 954 232 154
www.junta-andalucia.es/cultura
Open Wed. and Sat. 9am-8pm, Sun. 9am-2pm, Tues. and Thurs. 3-8pm.
Free entry for EU citizens.

This museum, dedicated to folklore and everyday life, was opened in 1972 and contains ceramics, examples of court dress and traditional costumes, original paintings of posters

2 Plaza de España ★★★

The Plaza de España was without doubt the star attraction of the 1929 Iberian–American Exhibition, and made the reputation of its architect, Aníbal González. The huge semi-circular square is an impressive sight and the towers at either end symbolise the power of the Catholic monarchs, Ferdinand and Isabella. Four bridges, representing the ancient Spanish kingdoms of Navarra, León, Castile and Aragón and decorated with ceramic tiles depicting the 58 Spanish provinces, span the surrounding moat.

advertising the spring festival and much more. In the basement, you can see reconstructions of Spanish houses from different periods of history, complete with furniture, as well as workshops including an instrument maker, potter, tanner and silversmith. Don't miss the ground-floor gallery which has the finest collection of peasant embroidery in Europe. (See p. 133.)

5 Plaza de América ★★

First started in 1916, the Plaza de América reflects the three main architectural styles most prevalent in Seville – Mudéjar, Renaissance and Gothic. The square is home to the former palace of antiquities (now the museum of folklore and arts), the archaeological museum, and the Royal pavilion, which houses the offices of the *Junta de Andalucía* (Andalucian Tourist Office), which were all designed by the architect Aníbal González.

6 Bilindo ★
Parque María Luisa
☎ 954 930 400
Open every day 8am–10pm.

Located opposite the Plaza de América, along the Paseo de las Delicias, this café is a welcome sight if you've been wandering through the park or have just trekked around the museums. The tables are set out against a backdrop of lush greenery, so take a break and get your energy back with a refreshing drink or some tasty tapas.

7 Museo Arqueológico ★★★
Plaza de América
☎ 954 232 401
   or 954 812 211
⊖ 954 629 542
www.junta-andalucia.es/cultura
Open Wed. and Sat. 9am-8pm, Sun. 9am-2pm, Tues. and Thurs. 3-8pm.
Free entry for EU citizens.

This museum is a must for all enthusiasts of archaeology and antiquity as it houses a superb collection of Roman statues and Spanish mosaics. If you simply appreciate beautiful objects, then don't miss the fabulous *Mosáico del Otoño*, (Mosaic of autumn), as well as the statues of Hermes, the Italic Venus and Diana the Hunter. (See p. 133.)

The Barrio de la Macarena, convents and churches

Though still very much part of the city, the Barrio de la Macarena has an almost village-like quality. The shops and bars along the Paseo de la Alameda de Hércules or the famous Calle de la Feria seem to belong to another era. This barrio, or district, famed for its religious traditions, is teeming with churches, convents and monasteries and is well known as home to the impassioned followers of the Virgen de la Macarena.

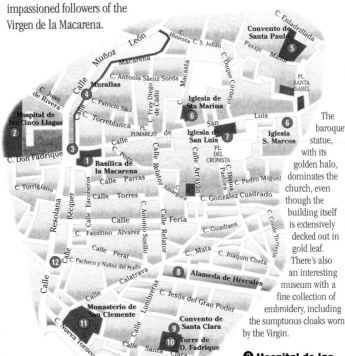

The baroque statue, with its golden halo, dominates the church, even though the building itself is extensively decked out in gold leaf. There's also an interesting museum with a fine collection of embroidery, including the sumptuous cloaks worn by the Virgin.

❶ Basílica de la Macarena★★
C. Bécquer, 1
☎ 954 370 195
or 954 901 800
Open every day 9.30am–1pm, 5-8pm.
Entry charge for the museum.

It's here you can find the Virgen de la Esperanza Macarena, the most famous and revered Virgin in the city.

❷ Hospital de las Cinco Llagas★★★
Entrance on C. Andueza
☎ 954 592 100
Visits by appointment.
Information available 8.30-10am, 5-7pm.

The 'Hospital of the Five Wounds' is one of the most beautiful examples of Renaissance architecture in Seville and was used to treat sailors who had returned from the Americas with unknown

PARLAMENTO

diseases. Since 28 February, 1992, the building has been the seat of the autonomous Andalucian Parliament. Its cruciform, neo-Classical church is now the chamber for plenary hearings.

❸ Puerta de la Macarena★

Just across from the Basilica stands the Puerta de la Macarena, an ochre and white painted gateway, the sole survivor of the sixteen gates that formed part of the city walls. Named by the Arabs after Princess Bab al-Makrina (who may have given her name to La Macarena), it was rebuilt in the 18th century incorporating what remained of the Islamic gate. It's easily recognisable from its huge pillars and the stunning tile-work picture of the Virgin.

❹ Murallas (city walls)★★
C. Andueza and C. Muñoz León.

It's not generally known that Seville was once the most strongly fortified city in Europe. Its original walls were built by Julius Caesar and further strengthened by the Arabs in 1147. The city was therefore able to boast a double defence, against enemy attacks and the River Guadalquivir's frequent floods.

❺ Convento de Santa Paula★★★
C. Santa Paula, 11
☎ 954 536 330
or 954 421 307
Open Tues.-Sun. 10.30am-12.30pm, 4.30-6.30pm.
Entry charge.

Many experts consider this royal monastery one of the

best examples of 15th-century religious architecture in Seville, furnished with dazzling altarpieces and statues. In the orchard there's a fine Gothic Mudéjar doorway, decorated with Renaissance-period tiles, which is a good example of the style known as 'Reyes Católicos' (Catholic Kings).

HEAVENLY DELIGHTS

The nuns that you can glimpse in convents across the city are engaged in a rather unusual activity for nuns — cooking.

They make a delicious array of cakes and confectionery from locally produced fruit, almonds, eggs and wine. These are on sale to the public at the entrances to some of the convents, and the best known, which has made the San Leandro convent famous, are *yemas*, a confection made from sugar and egg yolks (see p. 105). The nuns of the Santa Paula convent specialise in apricot preserve, while those of the San Clemente convent sell small cakes flavoured with white wine, vanilla or coconut. All of these heavenly temptations can be sampled at La Campana patisserie (see p. 78).

THE GREAT PROCESSION

Every year, during the Easter Week celebrations, the Basílica de la Macarena becomes a site of pilgrimage. Hundreds of followers gather round the famous statue and kneel before the high altar to venerate the Virgin in all her gleaming finery. At dawn on Good Friday, the statue is lifted onto the shoulders of a sinister-looking escort of penitents and paraded through the city streets to the cathedral.

❻ The Towers of San Marcos and Santa Marina★★

Just beyond the Puerta de la Macarena is the Calle San Luis. On the left-hand side of this street stand two magnificent towers, beautifully decorated with delicate filigree brickwork. They are the bell towers of the parish churches of San Marcos and Santa Marina and so resemble smaller versions of the Giralda that they are commonly called its 'sisters' or 'daughters'.

❼ Iglesia de San Luis★★

C. San Luis, on the corner with C. Divina
☎ 954 214 024
or 954 550 207
Open Wed. and Thurs. 9am-2pm, Fri. and Sat. 9am-2pm, 5-8pm.
Free entry.

On the right hand side of the street of the same name stands the extravagant baroque San Luis church. Founded in 1609 as a noviciate for the Society of Jesus (Jesuits), its façade is one of the city's most remarkable examples of baroque architecture, combining stone, brick and superb decorative sculpture in perfect proportion. The interior is equally fabulous and it's well worth taking time to enjoy the life-size painting by Zurbarán of St Louis, King of France, which forms the centrepiece of the high altar.

❽ Alameda de Hércules★

According to the words carved on the long since demolished Puerta de Jerez: 'Hercules built me, Julius Caesar surrounded me with walls and high towers'. This serves as a reminder that, nearing the end of the Roman

Republic, Andalucia was the main stage for the confrontation between Pompey and Caesar. Centuries later, towards the end of the 16th century, the marshland in the area was drained and a long boulevard was constructed on the reclaimed land. Today, it forms the site of a large fleamarket which takes place every Sunday and Thursday morning, and is a magnet for hundreds of Seville's bargain-hunters.

❾ Convento de Santa Clara★

C. Santa Clara, 40
☎ 954 379 905
The church can be visited on Saturdays at 7pm. Currently under restoration. Information available on request.

Almost hidden by the other buildings, you'll be able to spot this convent from the tile-work picture of St Clare of Assisi holding out a monstrance on its façade. When you've finished admiring the doorway and the altarpiece, take a look at the fine sculptures by Juan Martínez Montañés (1583–1627) of *Santa Clara*, the *Immaculate Conception* and *Christ Crucified*.

the lower floor and Gothic above. Like the majority of Seville's towers, the climb to the top is rewarded by fine views of the city.

⓫ Monasterio de San Clemente★★

C. Reposo, 9
☎ 954 379 905
Shop (pastries and ceramics) open 10am-1pm, 4-6pm. Convent open Mon.-Sat. 6-9pm, Sun. and public holidays noon-2pm. Free entry.

Right at the end of the Calle Santa Clara, at no. 91, you'll find the entrance to a church

while to take in the serenity of the vaulted cloister with its lush greenery and calm atmosphere. (See p. 124.)

⓬ Oromana

C. Resolana, 40
☎ 954 904 760

This old factory has been converted into a gallery housing a large collection of colonial-style furniture. You'll also find a selection of items for the home made from natural fibres from Asia, particularly Bali and the Philippines. Don't miss the opportunity to look around and perhaps pick up a few pretty decorative knick-knacks to fill up your suitcase – all at bargain prices.

❿ Torre de Don Fadrique★★

C. Santa Clara, 40
☎ 954 379 905
Open every day 11am-5.30pm. Currently under restoration. Information available on request.

In the second courtyard of the Santa Clara convent stands a tower that is so well preserved that it looks as if it's been reconstructed. However, it is totally original, and if you look carefully you'll notice that it has two contrasting styles of window designs – Romanesque on

that has been turned into a gallery for temporary exhibitions. Once the summer residence of the Moorish kings, it was transformed into a convent by King Fernando III in 1248. The building has undergone a number of modifications over the centuries and now nothing remains of its Islamic heritage. It's well worth pausing here a

The Barrio de San Vincente, the artists' quarter

Across the river from La Cartuja (see p. 63) lies the medieval quarter of San Vincente, which sprang up in the 16th century. Its ancient cobbled streets and elegant old-style houses with their belvederes and mosaic façades are a beautiful sight. And there's more to tempt you than just architecture – the superb Museo de Bellas Artes, second only to the Prado in Madrid as the finest art gallery in Spain, can also be found here.

[Map of the Barrio de San Vincente showing numbered locations: Iglesia de San Lorenzo y Jesús del Gran Poder (6), Iglesia de la Magdalena (4), Museo de Bellas Artes (1), and locations 2, 3, 5, 7, with streets including Jesús del Gran Poder, Calle Santa Ana, Teodosio, Calle San Miguel, Calle Jesús de la Veracruz, C. Vicente, Calle San Eloy, Plaza del Museo, etc.]

❶ Museo de Bellas Artes ★★★★

Plaza del Museo, 9
☎ 954 220 790
or 954 221 829
🖷 954 224 324
www.junta-andalucia.es/cultura
Open Tues. 3-8pm, Wed.-Sat. 9am-8pm, Sun. and public holidays 9am-3pm.
Free entry for EU citizens.

Since 1839, one of the world's finest collections of Spanish art has been housed in the baroque former Convento de la Merced. It includes works by some of Spain's greatest artists

including Murillo, Zurbarán, Velázquez and Valdés Leal. The old convent church displays a stunning collection of paintings by artists of the Golden Age, including Murillo's *Immaculate Conception*, and his remarkable *Virgin on a Napkin*, commissioned by Capuchin friars and painted, as the name suggests, on a table napkin. (See p. 126.)

❷ Monument to Murillo ★

Once you've visited the gallery, take a breather on one of the benches in the Plaza del Museo. In the middle of this romantic, tree-lined square stands a bronze statue of the painter Murillo – a tribute to the city's most celebrated artist. The monument symbolises the four principal disciplines of fine art – painting, sculpture, architecture, poetry and music.

3 CALLE SAN VINCENTE★

During the 18th and 19th centuries, the Calle San Vincente was one of the grandest streets in Seville. The splendid mansion that once belonged to the Marquis de Tablantes is now the Socialist Party headquarters. Further along, at no. 62, is the church of Santa María la Real and at no. 91, the Franciscan monastery of San Antonio de Padua. Walk on and you can see the San Vincente parish church which dates from the 13th century.

4 Iglesia de la Magdalena★★★

San Pablo, 10
☎ 954 229 603
Open Mon.-Sat. 7.30-11am, 6.30-9pm, Sun. 7.30am-1pm.

Recent restoration has given this beautiful baroque church a new lease of life, and the earthy reds and vibrant blue of its bell tower are now back to their former glory. The church is all that remains of what was once one of the most important convents in

Spain, the Convento de San Pablo. Unusually tall, with three naves, its artistic highlights include a mural by Lucas Valdés, bas-reliefs by Pedro Roldán and two superb paintings by Zurbarán.

5 El Hatillo★

C. Baños, 11
☎ 954 561 435
Open every day except Sun.
9am-2pm, 5.30-9pm.

As you head towards the Plaza de la Gavidia, on the street where the Turkish baths once stood, you'll find a delightful little shop on the right hand side. Its called the 'bundle' (*hatillo*), and that's just what it is – a bundle of fashionable stuff you won't find anywhere else. There are cuddly toys and other gadgets for the kids and accessories for trendy mums: sunglasses, pretty crochet swimsuits, handbags, hats and other creations from stylish Spanish designers.

6 Iglesia de San Lorenzo y Jesús del Gran Poder★★

Plaza San Lorenzo
☎ 954 384 558 or
954 385 454
Open every day 8am-1.45pm, 6-9pm
(Fri. 7.30am-10pm).

The church of San Lorenzo, in Gothic–Mudéjar style, stands in the square of the same name and is flanked by a superb 15th-century bell tower. Inside, near the choir,

is the huge *Virgin of Rocamadour* fresco, a significant work in the history of painting in Seville. The adjoining chapel contains a famous statue Jesús del Gran Poder (Jesus of Great Power), by Juan de Mesa, 1620.

7 Merchant★

C. Canalejas, 12
☎ 954 214 389

Not far from the church of La Magdalena this café-bar is just the place to quench your thirst at any time of the day. They can rustle up fabulous cocktails for you to sip outside, a very popular choice for the locals on a summer's evening. Occasionally you might even be invited to join in an impromptu improvised show.

Triana, the pulse of the city

On the bank of the Guadalquivir, opposite El Arenal, lies Triana, a district with a strong sense of identity. Locals will tell you that all the great bullfighters and exponents of flamenco were born here and the quarter exudes a permanentl' festive atmosphere, suffused with tradition and religious fervour. Triana draws its free, uninhibited nature from the smell of the sea wafting down the river.

and 72) is the perfect place to try some fish tapas. This street is also a good starting point for venturing off into the labyrinth of tiny roads that lead into the heart of Triana.

❶ Calle Betis★★★

This is one of the most beautiful streets in the Triana district (Betis being the old name for the Guadalquivir), and from here you get a fantastic view of the city. Any number of cool bars line the river bank. Take a seat at one of the terraces and enjoy the view of El Arenal. If you're feeling a mite peckish, the Kiosco de las Flores (see pp. 13

❷ Café de la Prensa★★

C. Betis, 8
☎ 954 333 420
Open every day 3pm-3am.

The walls of this café are covered in newspapers so

here's no shortage of topics
or conversation. Whether
ou're outside, overlooking
l Arenal, or inside, you'll
nd a warm atmosphere
erfect for playing games
uch as chess and cards. The
ouse specialities are well
orth trying (truffle tart,
pple tart, etc) and the music
imported direct from the
afé del Mar, the famous
ghtspot in Ibiza.

● El Rejoneo★
, Betis, 31b
pen Mon.-Sat. from 11pm.

iana is one of the areas that
ally come to life at night.
along the Calle Betis
rs line the bank of the
uadalquivir river. El Rejoneo
fers live entertainment,
t many people prefer to
outside enjoying the
chanting moonlight and
e reflection of the Torre del
o in the water.

❹ Puente Isabel II★★

This bridge is known locally
as the *Puente de Triana* as it
was the first to connect Seville
with the Triana quarter. Before
it was built in 1852, the
crossing had to be made on a
12th-century floating bridge
built by the Arabs. During
Holy Week, two legendary
religious confraternities, that
of the Esperanza Virgin and
the Christ of the Expiration,
known as El Cachorro, cross
this bridge on their way to the
cathedral. The sight of the two
statues reflected in the calm
waters at dawn is one of the
most stunning images of
Easter week in Seville.

❺ Plaza del Altozano★★

At one end of Calle
Betis lies the Plaza
del Altozano.
The houses on
this popular little
square have wrought-
iron *miradores*
(windows for spying
out) set into their
walls. During the
19th century the square
was a traditional
meeting place for
flamenco *cantaores*
(singers). The Taberna
de Berrinche, on the
corner of Calle
San Jorge and

CORRALES DE VECINOS

Literally meaning
'neighbourhood yards',
these adjoining houses were
built with all their rooms
looking out onto a single,
huge courtyard. This
central space served as a
communal living area
where neighbours would
wash, cook or even sing
and dance whenever the
party mood took them.
You can see several *corrales
de vecinos* along the Calle
Castilla, though the best
preserved is probably at
no. 16.

Calle San Jacinto is still a
popular hangout for artists
and bullfighters and in the
centre of the square stands a
statue of Triana's famous
bullfighting son, Juan
Belmonte.

❻ Callejón de la Inquisición★

If you follow the river
downstream along the
Calle Antillano Campos,
you come to the Callejón
de la Inquisición.
Centuries ago it
led up to the
imposing Castillo
San Jorge, where the
Spanish Inquisition
held its horrifying
trials. Heretics and
those accused of
witchcraft were
imprisoned in
the fortress,
many of them
preferring suicide to
the pitiless torment of
being burnt
at the
stake.

ALFARERÍA AND COMPANY

Triana is one of those areas with a little bit of everything. It's well-known for its pottery (*alfarería*) and ceramics of all kinds. Of the shops, the Cerámica Santa Ana (see p. 96), which is at no. 31 on Calle San Jorge, is probably the best-known. In Calle Alfareros, you'll find many studios where you can watch the craftsmen at work.

beautiful tortoiseshell cross which, according to legend, was a gift from some sailors rescued from a shipwreck.

❽ Capilla del Patrocinio★
C. Castilla, 182
Open every day 7-9pm.

This chapel contains one of the best examples of baroque sculpture in Seville – El Cachorro, the Christ of the Expiration (see no. 4, p. 59),

which has attained mythical status here. It shares the devotion of the people of Seville with the Jesús del Gran Poder. The sculptor took his inspiration from the face of a dying gypsy known as 'El Cachorro', after whom the statue is named.

❾ Sol y Sombra★★
C. Castilla, 151
☎ 954 333 935
Open Tues.-Sun (closed Tues. lunchtimes) 1-4pm, 8pm-midnight.

The walls of this typical little Andalucian establishment are covered with bullfighting posters and the ceiling is

hung with hams. It specialises in scrambled eggs with various meats as well as some excellent garlic roasted beef and *gambas al ajillo* (prawns in garlic).

❿ Iglesia de Santa Ana★★★
C. Pureza, 84
☎ 954 271 382
Open every day 9-11am, 7-9pm.

❼ Iglesia Nuestra Señora de la O★★
C. Castilla, 39
☎ 954 337 539
Open every day 9-11am, 7-9pm.

Easily recognised by its ochre-coloured bell tower with blue tiles, this baroque church was built in 1697. It contains a huge altarpiece of the eponymous Virgin and a remarkable composition by Pedro Roldán depicting St Anne, St Joachim and the Virgin and Child. Roldán's *Nazarene Christ* includes a

lfonso X El Sabio ('the Wise')
edicated this church to St
nne because she had cured
im of an eye infection. Once
he city's cathedral, it is now
place of pilgrimage for the
aithful from the religious
onfraternities of the district.
he high altar is dominated
y a magnificent Renaissance
ltarpiece. (See p. 123.)

⑪ Capilla de los
Marineros★★★
, Pureza, 53.

is little 17th-century chapel
ntains the Cristo de las Tres
aídas (three falls of Christ)
well as the famous Virgen
la Esperanza de Triana, the
eat rival of the Virgen de la
acarena for the hearts of
ville's religious faithful.
any given day you can see
mbers of locals kneeling in
votion before their beloved
rgin, bedecked in her golden
ery. Her doleful mystery is
the greater because it is
t known which artist was
sponsible for this beautiful
roque statue.

⑫ El Tejar★
C. San Jacinto, 68
☎ 954 344 487
Open every day 8.30am-3am.

This bar is a shrine to Triana,
where the owner was born.
He is assisted by a young chef
who is well versed in local
cooking and the result is an
original mix of traditional
cuisine and the personal
touch. If that isn't enough,
you can feast your eyes on an
exhibition of local culture.
There's a new one every
month.

⑬ Museo
de Carruajes★★
**Convento de los Remedios
Plaza de Cuba**
☎ 954 272 604
**Open every day 10am-2pm.
Entry charge.**

If you've had enough
of hearing
about
Seville's
religious
icons of Christ
and the Virgin,
and you've
explored every
inch of Calle Betis,
you'll find this
little museum a
refreshing change.
It contains fine displays

of 19th- and 20th- century
carriages with some unusual
audio-visual effects that bring
the history of this horse drawn
transport to life.

⑭ Cava
de San Jacinto★
C. San Jacinto, 90
☎ 954 333 735
**Open Mon.-Fri. 9am-
2.30pm, 5-9pm,
Sat. 9am-2.30pm.**

Cigar lovers will absolutely
adore this place. It boasts the
very latest humidifiers and
refrigeration systems so that
the cigars can bask in a
Cuban microclimate.
Unsurprisingly, you'll find a
large selection of Cuban as
well as Dominican and other
cigars for sale. If
you're not sure
what to buy,
just ask the
very helpful
staff.

Modern Seville, from the discovery of the Americas to Expo '92

After the successful 1992 Universal Exhibition, the vast space that it had occupied on the island of Cartuja was subject to a number of different proposals. The 'Cartuja 93' plan was launched to make use of the Exhibition's legacy, and Seville's greenest space has now been turned into a top class technological research park — a window on to the 21st century. However, its transformation is not yet complete and many buildings have yet to be restored to use. A trip on one of the double-decker buses that run around the island will give you an idea of how enormous the site is (see p. 33).

❶ Tecnopolis★

Tecnopolis incorporates a science and technology park as well as some departments of the university that are given over to research. It's hoped that the centre will become an authoritative point of reference in the future development of southern Europe. It includes highly advanced research centres, important laboratories and several major international bodies, all based here as part of an ambitious project developed by 'Cartuja 93'.

❷ Isla Mágica★★

Isla de la Cartjua
Pabellón de España
☎ 902 161 716
(information)
or 902 160 000
(bookings)
www.islamagica.es
Prices and times are very variable. It's essential to phone for the latest information and book in advance.

A visit to the 'Magic Island' is a really fun way of learning about Seville's history, taking you back to the 16th-century city as well as the voyages of the New World explorers. There's plenty to do at this theme park that will delight both grown-ups and children alike. There are gigantic roller coasters (the most famous is the 'Jaguar'), tropical riverboat rides and excellent live shows. One of

he latest attractions to open
the Planetarium, the first
60° cinema of its kind in
urope, which opened its
oors in 2001.

❷ Espacio Cultural Puerta Triana★★

Unfortunately, this part of
the complex is closed at the
moment, as it has not proved
easy to decide what
should be done
with it.

**Monasterio
de Santa María
de las Cuevas**

❺ Cartuja

**❸ Espace Culturel
Puerta de Triana**

III

eople have suggested that
e boats displayed along the
ank here spoil the view of the
ver, but negotiations about
e future of the site are
going. It's hoped to reopen
e nautical pavilion, which
fered a fascinating glimpse
Seville's history, and the
citing cinematic experience
the Omnimax, one of
urope's biggest in-the-round
eatres.

❹ Parque del Alamillo★★

**Winter: open every day
8am-8pm; summer: open
every day 8am-2am.**

This 894,000-sq m (221-
acre) park is the city's
main green space. Due
to a strict programme
of reforestation and the
constant introduction of
new species, the park offers
visitors a glimpse of the
Mediterranean's diverse
ecosystem. El Amalillo,
however, is not just about the
environment. There are plenty
of opportunities for cultural
and sporting activities, as well
as places to eat and drink
and even to hire a bicycle to
help you get around.

❺ La Cartuja Nuestra Señora Santa María de las Cuevas★★★

**Isla de la Cartuja
☎ 954 480 611
✆ 954 480 612
Summer (1 April-30 Sept.):
open Tues.-Sun., public
holidays and days preceding
public holidays, 11am-9pm.
Winter (1 Oct-31 Mar.):
open Tues.-Sun., public
holidays and days preceding
public holidays, 11am-7pm.
Entry charge.**

This beautiful building is part
of the city's great architectural
heritage. At the beginning of

Six brand new bridges
were built over the
Guadalquivir river for the
Universal Exhibition of
1992. These modern
architectural monuments
were built using the most
advanced engineering
available at the time.
The highest is the
impressive Puente del
Centenario, while the
Alamillo, designed by
Santiago de Calatrava,
is the only bridge in the
world to have its whole
weight supported by a
single pillar.

the 15th century, La Cartuja
started its life as a Carthusian
monastery. Later, it was
converted into the famous
Cartuja de Sevilla ceramics
factory and it's now used as
an artistic and cultural
centre, shared by several
different institutions.

Rooms and restaurants
Practicalities

The selection of hotel accommodation in Seville has improved vastly since Expo '92. Today, a varied range of accommodation can be found in the city, including all the usual chains. You can enjoy every comfort in one of the big luxury hotels, choose one of the charming smaller hotels, or plump for a clean, centrally located guesthouse. Whatever your fancy, it's not hard to find a good room at a reasonable rate.

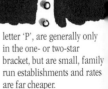

HOTELS

CHOOSING A HOTEL

Seville is proud of its reputation as a tourist city, and the list of hotels is extensive. A comfortable room conveniently located near the city centre or the Barrio de Santa Cruz can usually be found at a reasonable price.

Hotels are classified by the local authorities who award them from one to five stars according to the facilities on offer (rather than the levels of service) and it's quite possible to find a charming hotel with impeccable service but only three stars. The *pensiones* (guest houses), denoted by the

letter 'P', are generally only in the one- or two-star bracket, but are small, family run establishments and rates are far cheaper.

THE PARADORS OF SPAIN

The *paradores* are a network of state-run, top of the range hotels set in superbly restored castles, palaces, monasteries etc. Facilities are generally excellent and the service superb. Prices vary but, as a rule, they are all fairly pricey. A double room costs around €125 (including breakfast), but rates are lower at the weekends and in the low season. The Parador Alcázar

del Rey Don Pedro (☎ 954 141 010 🅕 954 141 712, email: carmona@parador.es), is located in the ancient town of Carmona, 38 km (24 miles) east of Seville, with 10 daily bus services from the city. It's set high in the old part of the town and is one of the most beautiful hotels in the parador network, housed in a Moorish fortress converted into a palace by King Pedro the Cruel. With lovely gardens, restaurant, pool and wonderful views over the

plains below, its flower-clad patio is a perfect spot for a drink. If you can't afford to spend the night in a parador, you can still enjoy the location by eating in their restaurants, where they serve high quality regional cuisine. You'll need to book ahead in summer and at weekends.
Website: www.parador.es

Keytel International
404 Edgware Road
London W2 1ED
☎/🅕 020 7616 0300

PRICES

On average you should allow between €35 and €75 for a double room, although during Easter Week and the Feria prices can double.

BOOKING

The most difficult times to find accommodation are during Easter week and the April Feria. Bookings for these times should ideally be made well in advance. You can make your reservation by fax or by post direct to the hotel and you'll only be asked to pay a deposit, most likely by credit card.

RESTAURANTS

Eating well is an essential part of life in Seville. The city has hundreds of restaurants where you can enjoy the simple delights of a huge variety of local specialities – reflecting Seville's many different cultural traditions. Meat and fish are particularly well prepared. Some of the more sophisticated restaurants specialise in Basque food, which may seem surprising at this end of the country – but is an opportunity to try a

very different cuisine. A true Andalucian tradition is a tapas evening. As you wander from bar to bar you can sample the famous *salmorejo* (tomato-based salsa), crispy *pescaíto frito* (fried fish) or a delicious *gazpacho* (cold tomato soup). If you need extra help, there's a guide, *Tapeando por Sevilla*, which lists the best places in each area and is available from Tourist Offices and some bars.

MEALTIMES

Throughout Spain and especially in Seville, mealtimes tend to differ by up to a couple of hours from what you may be used to in the UK. The exception is breakfast which, as you might expect, is around 8am, before people head off for work. At 11am there's

traditionally a little break for a coffee and a *tostada* (piece of toast) or a *pincho de tortilla* (slice of omelette), to tide you over until lunchtime (especially welcome if you've missed breakfast to enjoy an extra half-hour in bed!). Restaurants open for lunch from 1pm, but Spaniards don't eat before 2 or even 3pm. You can normally get served until 4pm, but in most tourist areas you'll find bars that stay open all day. *La merienda* (tea) at 6pm will keep you going until dinner, which is served in restaurants from 8.30pm – but you won't be surprised to learn that most Spaniards don't sit down for dinner until after 10pm.

PRICES

In general, eating out is good value, even if you're determined to try out some of the bars in the city centre (though it's best to avoid the really touristy places). Tapas can be an economical way of trying the local dishes. In the restaurants, the slightly higher prices tend to reflect the better quality of the food, and you can usually find something to suit all tastes. At lunchtime, most restaurants offer a *menú del día* (set menu of the day), which is usually an attractively priced, three-course meal.

HOTELS

Around the university

Alfonso XIII★★★★★

San Fernando, 2
☎ 954 917 000
🖶 954 917 099
www.westin.com

Decorated with marble and tiles, this sumptuous Moorish-style palace was built for the 1929 Exhibition. The furniture, paintings and chandeliers are worthy of royalty and the luxurious standard of the richly decorated rooms has guaranteed a stream of famous guests.

El Centro

Melia Colón Hotel★★★★★

C. Canalejas, 1
☎ 954 222 900
🖶 954 220 938
www.solmelia.com

The classic elegance of this central hotel is both luxurious and comfortable. It is strongly associated with bullfighting as the *toreros* depart from here on their way to the Maestranza bullring. The rooms on the upper levels have stupendous views and its restaurant, El Burladero (see p. 73) is considered one of the best in town.

Casa Imperial★★★★★

C. Imperial, 29
☎ 954 500 300
🖶 954 500 330
www.casaimperial.com

This 16th-century stately home once belonged to the butler of the first Marquis of Tarifa, who owned the Casa de Pilatos. You can relax and enjoy the refreshing fountains in one of several courtyards. The rooms are tastefully decorated and each has its own private little patio as well as a small kitchen.

Taberna del Alabardero★★★★

C. Zaragoza, 20
☎ 954 560 637
or 954 502 721
🖶 954 563 666
hotel.alabardero@esh.es

This 19th-century mansion has seven suites named after the

seven provinces of Andalucia, all richly decorated with period furnishings. The Taberna del Alabardero is the headquarters of Seville's Hotel School and offers a choice of several restaurants with a wide range of culinary styles (see p. 72). Lunch, which is normally prepared by the students, is excellent value. Other attractions include concerts and painting exhibitions.

Las Casas del Rey de Baeza★★★

C. Santiago, 2
☎ 954 561 496
🖶 954 561 441
baeza@zoom.es

This charming hotel, a stone's throw from the Casa de Pilatos, was converted from an old 'neighbourhood yard' (see p. 59). It combines traditional elements with the modern comforts you'd expect from a chic hotel – carefully designed interiors and impeccable service. Parking, swimming pool and solarium are all available.

Las Casas de los Mercaderes★★★

C. Alvárez Quintero, 9–13
☎ 954 225 858
🖶 954 229 884
mercaderes@zoom.es

This hotel has a very peaceful atmosphere despite its location right in the heart of the city business centre. Built around a remarkable 18th-century courtyard, the comfortable rooms are oases of calm. Private parking.

Residencia Londres★★
C. Pedro Mártir, 1
☎ 954 212 896

This hotel, situated in a quiet city-centre street, is a Sevillian townhouse built at the beginning of the 19th century and restored using traditional Andalucian ceramics. The rooms are simply but comfortably furnished, and offer excellent value for money.

Baco★★
Plaza Ponce de León, 15
☎ 954 565 050
📠 954 563 654

This hotel, which stands opposite the Santa Catalina Church, is of considerable artistic interest. Its restaurant, El Bacalao, specialises, as its name suggests, in *bacalao* (cod).

Plaza Sevilla★
C. Canalejas, 2
☎ 954 217 149
954 221 904

This small hotel, built in early 20th-century regional style, is near the Museo de Bellas Artes (see p. 56). Designed by architect Aníbal González, it's a *típico* (traditional) building and

the rooms, though unpretentious, are generous in size and very comfortable.

Santa Cruz

Vincent Van Gogh★★
C. Miguel Mañara, 4
☎ 954 563 727

Located within a short walk of the cathedral, this attractive, early 20th-century building has recently been renovated. The rooms all have TVs and spotless bathrooms, and those overlooking the courtyard have wrought iron *miradores*. Try and avoid the ground-floor rooms overlooking the courtyard, however, as they tend to be a little on the dark side.

Picasso★★
C. San Gregorio, 1
☎/📠 954 210 864
hpicasso@arrakis.es

This hotel is run by the same owners as the Vincent Van Gogh, and the views of the cathedral from the balconies are breathtaking. Its standards are just as high as the Van Gogh but it's a little noisier.

Goya★
C. Mateos Gago, 31
☎ 954 211 170
📠 954 562 988

This typical Sevillian house, spotlessly presented, is one of those rare hotels whose tariffs remain the same all year round. It's a charming little establishment right in the centre of the Santa Cruz district, offering excellent value for money and a warm welcome in true Sevillian style.

Doña María★★★★

C. Don Remondo, 19
☎ 954 224 990
🅕 954 219 546
reserves@hdmaria.com
www.hdmaria.com

Great location, comfort and elegant interiors are the qualities of this well-known hotel. Located in the heart of Seville's historic centre, its rooms are all named after famous Sevillians. There's an open-air bar on the roof with a swimming pool, perfect for enjoying a drink overlooking the Giralda.

Los Seises★★★★

C. Segovia, 6
☎ 954 229 495
🅕 954 224 334
www.sol.com/hotel-los-seises

Los Seises

This hotel forms part of the Palacio Arzobispal (archbishop's palace) and is cosily set around its third courtyard. It combines the old (Renaissance ceilings, tiles and Roman mosaics) with the ultramodern. Its restaurant is considered one of the best in Seville and the view from the outdoor pool is magnificent.

Las Casas de la Judería★★★

Callejón de Dos Hermanas, 7
☎ 954 415 150
🅕 954 422 170
www.lascasas.zoom.es

This superb hotel consists of an entire group of traditional Sevillian houses. The *albero* colour of the walls (the yellow of the sand in the bullring) and its flower-decked courtyards give the beautifully preserved complex a sunny brightness. The rooms are very comfortable and tastefully decorated.

Barrio de San Vincente

Roma★★

C. Gravina, 34
☎954 501 300
🅕 954 501 301

This newly opened hotel is liberally decorated with tiles and wrought iron. It's located right by the Museo de Bellas Artes with very individually furnished and unfussily decorated rooms. Those overlooking the street are double-glazed.

Zaida★

C. San Roque, 26
☎ 954 211 138
🅕 954 903 624

This hotel offers Mudéjar-style décor in an18th-century *casa palacio* located in a very quiet street. The rooms are comfortable and air-conditioned.

Barrio de la Macarena

San Gil★★★

C. Parras, 28
☎ 954 906 811
🅕 954 906 939

Located near the Basílica de la Macarena, this listed early 20th-century building is one of the prettiest in the city. It's typically Sevillian, with a courtyard garden, *azulejo*-decked walls and wrought iron gates. On the upper level, there's a delightful outdoor swimming pool.

Patio de la Cartuja★★★

C. Lumbreras, 8–10
☎ 954 900 200
𝐅 954 902 056
patios@bbv.net

This hotel offers the opportunity to stay in a former 'neighbourhood house' (see p. 59). The rooms open off a long corridor that overlooks a courtyard and each one has a sitting room and tiny kitchen.

. Corregidor★★★

. Morgado, 17
☎ 954 385 111
𝐅 954 384 238

Hidden down a little side street near the Alameda de Hércules,

this is a typical Andalucian-style building. The hotel is very quiet and the bright, spacious rooms look out onto beautiful flower-filled courtyards.

Patio de la Alameda★★★

Alameda de Hércules, 56
☎ 954 904 999
𝐅 954 900 226
patios@bbvnet.com

This hotel, which was once La Montaña hospital, is arranged around three courtyards. It's extremely bright and colourful, with ochre walls and blue mouldings. A mix of traditional style, modern comfort and genial service combine to relax and revive the weary traveller.

Simón★

C. García de Vinuesa, 19
☎ 954 226 660
or 954 226 615
𝐅 954 562 241

Every nook and cranny of this 18th-century palace conceals a reminder of the past. With its antique furniture, the hotel is steeped in Andalucian romance and tradition. Book well ahead as its charming rooms are very reasonably priced.

Monte Triana★★★

C. Clara de Jesús Montero, 24
☎954 341 111
or 954 085 000
𝐅 954 343 328
htmreservas@hotelesmonte.
com

Comfort and practicality mark out this hotel, which is located off the usual tourist trail but nevertheless still only five minutes from the city centre. You're in Seville, so of course it has the obligatory courtyard.

Barceló Gran Hotel Renacimiento★★★★★

Isla de la Cartuja
☎ 954 462 222
𝐅 954 460 428
www.barcelo.com

This huge hotel is one of the most modern in Seville, built within the walls of the old Cartuja monastery for Expo '92. Furnished with every conceivable hi-tech feature, and all the comforts you could wish for, it's a perfect place for winding down away from the hustle and bustle of the city.

Corregidor hotel

RESTAURANTS

Centro

Casa Robles★★★★

C. Alvarez Quintero, 58
☎ 954 563 272
or 954 213 150
🄵 954 564 479
www.casa-robles.com
Open every day 1-5pm,
8.30pm-1am.
Booking
recommended.

This establishment,
founded in 1954, is
forever fashionable
and has earned
almost mythical
status in Seville.
Its delights simply
have to be experi-
enced and clients
include professionals,
families celebrating a
major event or visitors keen
to discover the latest culinary

twist given to local recipes. As
well as the excellent grilled meat
and fish, there's a choice of over
30 different specialities. Yet some
do stand out – duck's liver with
preserves from the Santa Paula
convent or the entrecôte *à la
sevillana*, not to mention the
delicious pastries. The tapas are

also to be relished, accompanied
by a glass of local wine. It's
equally pleasant whether you're
sitting outside or inside, in the
typically Sevillian setting with
traditional colours and ceramics.

Eneldo★★★★

C. Perez Galdos, 20
☎ 954 501 356
Booking recommended.

At the back of this typical
Sevillian house, located a stone's
throw from the Plaza del Alfalfa,
is the motto: 'Eat well for well-
being'. This new restaurant, run
by a young, dynamic team,
offers an excellent selection of
dishes served in a cheerful
setting, comfortably decked out
with designer furniture, while
retaining its original mirrors and
chandeliers. The chef, Alvaro
Morales, takes his inspiration
from the finest exponents of the
culinary arts, building on their
knowledge to stimulate his
own creative ideas. Every day
he seems to come up with more
delicately presented and highly
flavoured dishes, using meat and
fish that are both tender and
fresh. One of the most innovative restaurants in the city.

Mesón Don Raimundo★★★

C. Argote de Molina, 26
☎ 954 223 355
or 954 212 925
🄵 954 218 951
Open every day, noon-
5pm, 7pm-midnight.
Booking
recommended.

This former 14th-century
convent lies hidden at the
end of a side street behind
the Palacio Arzobispal.
Richly decorated and furnished with antique furniture,
tapestries and pictures, it looks
more like a museum than

restaurant. Its historic charm has become the stuff of legend, as have its wine cellar and authentic Andalucian cooking. This is not mere chance as the owner, Raimundo Fernandez, has received several awards for preserving a fast disappearing culinary heritage. Every day his ovens are filled with traditional dishes from Seville, Huelva and Cádiz made from age-old recipes that have been all but forgotten. Here you can rediscover the delights of Mozarabic cuisine, especially the desserts, as well as authentic *tortillas* (omelettes).

Barrio de Santa Cruz

El Modesto★★

C. Cano y Cueto, 5 (Puerta de la Carne)
☎ 954 416 811
or 954 411 816
✆ 954 922 502
www.grupomodesto.com
Open every day 8am-2am.

Near the Murillo gardens, on the Plaza de los Refinadores, you'll find this delightful restaurant. Laid out on two floors, it's renowned for its excellent service and quality food – particularly the impressive array of fried fish and shellfish. Come spring, you can dine outside on the serene terrace on the square,

La Judería

which boasts a statue of Don Juan and is fringed with palms and orange-trees.

La Judería★★

C. Cano y Cueto, 13
☎ 954 412 052
or 954 426 456
✆ 954 902 502
Open every day 12.30-5pm,
7.30pm-12.30am.

As its name suggests, this restaurant is located right in the middle of the Jewish quarter. The dining room, however, couldn't be more Andalucian in style, with bricks and fired-earth floor tiles. The food isn't particularly Jewish either, as the restaurant specialises in grilled and fried fish and other seafood, especially good shell-fish, all washed down with Aljarafe wine. If you could only try one dish, it would have to be the *casuela de arroz con mariscos* (seafood with saffron

rice). A meal here costs around €25 unless you opt for the tourist menu at €12.

La Albahaca★★

Plaza de Santa Cruz,12
☎ 954 220 714
or 954 560 014
✆ 954 561 204
www.Andalunet.com/
la-albahaca
Open Mon.-Sat. noon-4pm,
8pm-midnight.

Superior service complements excellent food from a strongly seasonal menu. This charming restaurant, spread over three separate rooms of a beautiful house, is romantically furnished with 17th-century and early 20th-century antiques. It's an ideal setting for a candle-lit dinner for two. You can eat inside or, in summer, outside in the lovely square – where you can enjoy delicious and beauti-fully-presented Andalucian and Basque cuisine.

La Albahaca

Triana

Kiosco de las Flores★★★

C. del Betis
☎ 954 333 898
or 954 274 576
Open Tues.-Sun. noon-
11.30pm.

You can't miss this delightful white-painted brick kiosk on the Guadalquivir river, not far from the Plaza de Cuba end of the Calle Betis. With a fine view across to the Torre del Oro, there's rarely space to sit down outside until after 4pm. There's a huge choice of fried fish at lunchtime – whitebait, fresh anchovies, squid, shrimps and prawns, red mullet, hake ... Take your pick!

Around the university

Egaña Oriza★★★★

C. San Fernando, 41
☎ 954 227 254
or 954 227 211
🖷 954 502 727
Open Mon.-Fri. 1.30-4pm,
9pm-midnight.
Booking essential in high
season.

This is one of a chain of very stylish restaurants found all over Spain. The cool, bright dining room, decked out in pale wood with a glass roof, quickly fills up in the tourist season. The menu offers a choice of Basque and

Sevillian specialities made with seasonal meats, fish and fresh vegetables. The combination of Andalucian produce and savoir-faire from the north of Spain results in a colourful and highly flavoured cuisine. The fillet of hake in green sauce is very good and the *angulas* (tiny eels) are succulent – though be warned, the bill can be a little steep at around €30.

El Arenal

Taberna del Alabardero★★★★

C. Zaragoza, 20
☎ 954 560 637
or 954 502 721
🖷 954 563 666
Open every day 1.30pm-
4pm, 8.30pm-12.30am.

Faithfully restored in period style, this charming 19th-century mansion was once owned by poet J. Antonio Cavestany, a member of the Spanish Royal Academy, and its romantic atmosphere retains some of his poetic spirit. There's been a Hotel School here for over twenty years and the restaurant, under the direction of head chef, Juan Manuel Marcos, is excellent value, the food naturally being of a high standard. There's a bar and tea can be taken outside in the

Egaña Oriza

courtyard. After your meal, it's well worth taking a walk on the terrace, which has a very pretty view of the Giralda.

El Burladero★★

C. Canalejas, 1
☎ 954 222 900
❻ 954 220 938
Open every day 1.30-4pm, 9pm-midnight.

Located next to the church of La Magdalena, this restaurant was opened in 1989 as part of the bullfighters' very own hotel, the Melia Colón (see p. 66). The *burladero* is the barrier that runs around the inside of the bullring so, needless to say, the ambiance is one hundred per cent bullfight-dominated. It's an institution in Seville and very dear to the hearts of bullfighting fans. The menu offers traditional local recipes, including Andalucian-style hake and, of course, the famous bull's tail. Tapas fanatics are also well catered for.

Barrio de la Macarena

Don Fadrique★

C. Don Fadrique, 7-9
☎ 954 904 000
or 954 377 801
❻ 954 904 000
donfadrique@retemail.es
Open every day noon-4.30pm, 8pm-2am.

The food in this restaurant, located between the Puerta de la Macarena and the Andalucian Parliament, is good honest fare and a set meal costs around €10. The service is excellent and the décor slightly kitsch, with private dining rooms for business lunches. The cellar has a fine range of wines and the specialities, both regional and national, are first-rate.

Outside the city walls

Le Florencia★★★

Av. de Eduardo Dato, 49
☎ 954 548 300
❻ 954 532 342
Open Mon.-Sat. 1.30-4pm, 9pm-2am.

The Florencia forms part of the Porta Coeli hotel, located in the city's more modern business district. It has a very welcoming ambiance and enjoys

an excellent reputation throughout the city. Considered one of the best restaurants in Seville, it offers a combination of fine national and international cuisine, with superb fish and meat dishes and a regularly changing menu.

Taberna Medieval★

Av. Concejal Alberto Jimenez Becerril (near Barqueta bridge)
☎ 954 907 951
Open Tues.-Sun. noon-midnight.

As you may have already guessed, this 'tavern' offers a medieval-style experience. The starters are all typical dishes from the mountain regions and the plates of beef are served in impressively generous chunks. Apart from beef, there's venison, wild boar, black pudding, horsemeat, ostrich and even 'fighting bull', all served with a first-class choice of regional wines and *oloroso* or *fino* sherries from Jerez. The atmosphere is rustic and affable and the price per person comes to around €21.

TAPAS BARS

Ir de tapeo (going on a tapas 'crawl') is one of the most enjoyable ways of eating in Seville. The choice of bars is fantastic and you can experience quite a number without having to walk very far. If you see the sign 'tourist bar' then (unlike a restaurant) it doesn't necessarily mean you're going to get ripped off – the quality is usually pretty good. If you stick to the selection of bars given here you won't go too far wrong – but it shouldn't stop you from trying out any bar that takes your fancy.

El Centro

Habanita

C. Golfo, 3
☎ 954 219 516
www.andalunet.com/habanita
Open every day 12.30-4.30pm, 8.30pm012.30am.

With exotic surroundings and a genial atmosphere, this café offers a good range of vegetarian Mediterranean specialities. Washed down with Cuban-style cocktails, they are perfect for satisfying a rumbling stomach.

The homemade chocolate cakes are particularly good.

Bar Estrella

C. Estrella, 3
☎ 954 561 426
Open Mon.-Sat.
9 am-midnight.

This small local bar has earned itself a reputation as the quintessential place for a tapas experience. Located right in the city centre, it's highly popular with Sevillians who know the right places to go. In fine weather you can soak up the lively atmosphere at one of the tables that run the length of the street and treat yourself to homemade

pâté, fried fish or *croquetas de la casa* (homemade potato croquettes).

Enrique Becerra

C. Gamazo, 2
☎ 954 213 049
🖷 954 227 093
26mayo98@suq.servicom.es
Open Mon.-Fri. 1-5pm,
8pm-midnight.

This traditional Andalucian bar serves tapas but also has a restaurant on the first floor. Popular with locals, its location and great atmosphere make it very much part of the lively city-centre scene and a really good first port of call before you venture off to other bars. Try the smoked tuna with tomatoes or *calderilla* (beef in sauce).

Europa

C. Siete Revueltas, 35
☎ 954 221 354
Open Sun.-Wed. 8am-noon,
Thurs.-Sat. 8am-1am.

This bar was first opened in 1925 and has recently been taken over and restored by three young architects. They serve a range of breakfasts and tapas from 8am.

Habanita

Europa

You can eat indoors (pleasant décor) or at one of the tables outside on the Plaza del Pan, overlooking San Salvador church. All the tapas are delicious but the partridge pâté is an absolute must and the tapa of the day is always worth a try.

Becerrita

C. Recaredo, 9
☎ 954 412 057
☎ 954 533 727
becerrita@andalunet.com
Open Mon.-Sat. 12.30-4.30pm, 8pm-12.30am,
Sun. 12.30-4.30pm.

Jesús María Becerra, the son of Enrique Becerra (see p. 74), opened his own

place in 1988. Heavily involved in the numerous gastronomic events that promote Andalucian cuisine, he explores new possibilities by adapting traditional recipes to create highly imaginative tapas such as *croquetas de cola de toro* (bull's tail croquettes), *chocos en su tinta con arroz* (cuttle-fish in their own ink with rice), *revuelto de papas con chorizo* (scrambled eggs with potato and chorizo sausage). It's impossible to describe them all, so you'll just have to find out for yourself!

Cervecería Internacional

C. Gamazo, 3
☎ 954 211 717
Open Mon.-Sat. noon-4pm, 8pm-midnight.

Beer enthusiasts will feel completely at home here, with a choice of 15 draught beers from all over the world and over 200 bottled beers. Though the drinks are anything but typical, the tapas, rest assured, are the real thing. The shrimp salad is justifiably famous and well worth a go.

Casablanca

C. Zaragoza, 50
☎ 954 224 698
Open Mon.-Sat. 12.30-5pm, 8pm-midnight.

Everyone visits this bar – even the King of Spain has been here. If you want to follow the royal example, start with the *papas aliñás* (spicy potatoes). They do excellent fish here, including Andalucian specialities such as *salmorejo* and a wonderful *tortilla de patatas al whisky* (potato omelette with whisky). If you can't decide, Don Manuel, the owner will be happy to help you choose.

Picalagartos

C. Hernando Colón, 7
☎ 954 226 940
Open every day 4pm-2.30am.

Locals love to gather in this lively café before heading off on a tour of the rest of the bars. It's also a favourite place to spend a quiet afternoon chatting with friends or playing cards or chess.

Barrio de Santa Cruz

Las Teresas

C. Ximénez Enciso, 1
☎ 954 213 069
Open every day 9.30am-4pm, 8pm-midnight.

Located right in the heart of the Santa Cruz quarter, this small Sevillian bar is naturally very popular with tourists. It's certainly a good place to take a rest, whether you sit inside or out. The specialities of the house, including various charcuterie from Huelva and Salamanca, are excellent, as is the traditional home cooking.

Casa Román

Plaza de los Venerables, 1
☎ 954 228 483
or 954 216 408
Open Mon.-Sat. 9.30am-
4pm, 7pm-midnight,
Sun. 11am-4pm.

Stop off and try the *jamón ibérico* (Iberian ham) or savour homemade tapas in the bar's colourful atmosphere and picturesque surroundings. If you can, sit outside, and admire the bougainvillea on the balconies of the white houses all around.

La Andana

C. Argote de Molina
☎ 954 213 150
✆ 954 564 479
Open every day
noon-midnight.

Located right by the cathedral, this is another perpetually lively bar that is great for tapas. There's a huge selection of *montaditos* – hot bread rolls stuffed with *morcilla* (black pudding), *lomo* (pork), or chorizo – to enjoy outside in the summer sun.

Casa Morales

Altamira

C. Santa María la Blanca, 4
☎ 954 425 030
Open every day 8am-
midnight.

There can be few things more pleasant in Seville than having a drink outside this bar or munching your way through a selection of their tapas. Specialities include *pescaíto frito* (fried fish), spinach with pine nuts and bull's tail.

El Arenal

Casa Morales

C. García de Vinuesa, 11
☎ 954 221 242
Open Mon.-Sat. noon-4pm,
8pm-midnight.

This bar, founded in 1850, is still owned by the same family. They offer a selection of classic tapas for you to try and some great *montaditos*.

Mesón de la Infanta

Abacería del Postigo

C. Tomás de Ibarra, 4
☎ 954 229 336
Open Mon.-Sat. 5.30am-5pm, 8pm-1am.

If you like trying local wines, visit the Abacería del Postigo and taste selections from Rioja, Ribera del Duero and Somontano, along with a variety of cheeses, charcuterie and tapas. The tapas change according to what's available in the market, but can include *chipirones en su tinta* (squid in its own ink), and *lomo a la mozarabe con frutos secos* (Mozarabic-style loin of pork with dried fruit). You can also buy excellent local produce to take home.

Esquinita de Arfe

C. Arfe, 26
Open every day
9am-4pm, 7-11pm.

This small, family-run restaurant, popular with the locals, is quite an intimate experience – so don't tell everyone about it! You can lunch on the set-price menu of the day, which is good value, and once a week, they cook up a special dish for the whole restaurant. Everything is homemade, of course.

Mesón de la Infanta

C. Dos de Mayo, 26
☎ 954 561 554
or 954 221 909
Open every day except Tues.
12.30-4pm, 7pm-midnight.

Situated close to the Maestranza bullring, this is where people like to meet up after a bullfight. You can stand at the bar to try some of the tapas or take refuge in the relative calm of the restaurant. There's also a little shop

selling local produce. All the tapas are excellent, but if you're having lunch, ask for the dish of the day. If you really want to push the boat out, order the *jamón Serrano* (Serrano ham), which is delicate and notoriously difficult to carve – it's an acquired skill and is very impressive to watch.

Eslava

C. Eslava, 5
☎ 954 906 568
Open Mon.-Sat. 1.30-5.30pm, 9pm-midnight,
Sun. 1.30-5.30pm.

This little bar, located in San Vincente, is a very trendy hangout for Seville's younger crowd. The décor is modern but the savoir faire is classic. The authentic tapas are a feat of creative endeavour and it's packed at weekends, when it really comes to life. The restaurant, next door, offers an excellent selection of international cuisine.

Triana

Antigua Taberna la Cava

C. Pagés del Corro, 93
☎ 954 330 120

Step into this bar and you're immediately transported back to 18th-century Seville, a time when peasants and gypsies gathered together to sing *soleas* or *seguidillas*. More importantly, it's a chance to try some delicious cheeses and excellent meats – the *ibérico* ham served with fresh bread, baked on the premises, is a joy to savour.

TEAROOMS

El Centro

Rayas

C. Almirante Apodaca, 1
(Plaza de San Pedro)
☎ 954 221 746

Most ice cream parlours get busy just before 6pm, after the daily siesta, and this is no exception. It's an institution in Seville and has recently further broadened its appeal by specialising in chocolates as well. You can splurge out on exquisite ice creams and homemade almond slices or take home an appetising box of dark or milk chocolates.

La Campana

C. Sierpes, 1-3
☎ 954 223 570
Open every day 8am-10pm.

On the Plaza de la Campana, at the corner of Calle Martín Villa, the pavement is covered with tables belonging to the biggest patisserie in Seville. In business since 1885, La Campana has established a firm reputation as one of Seville's most celebrated cafés. It specialises in delicious pastries for *merienda* (teatime), and offers numerous handmade specialities, many created by nuns from the city's convents. Temptations include ice creams, *torrijas* (bread soaked in milk and honey then fried), *yemas de San Leandro* (see p. 105), *peces de nata* (cream cakes), *tocino de cielo* (strawberry cream cake) and homemade rum babas known as *borrachos* (drunkards), though you'd need to eat quite a few to feel any real effect!

Ochoa

C. Sierpes, 45
☎ 954 225 528
Av. de la República
Argentina, 21
☎ 954 276 417
C. Virgen de Lujan, 22
☎ 954 279 060

This tearoom is also a patisserie and confectioners and is the top choice for milkshakes – they make the best in Seville – and *medianoches*, succulent little bread rolls filled with butter and ham. They have been making ice creams and sorbets here since 1910 using simple, quality ingredients, so give in to the sweet temptation and choose from such flavours as chocolate, pistachio, nougat and raspberry.

Abades

C. Abades, 13
☎ 954 225 622
Open every day from 4pm until dawn.

Located behind the Palacio Arzobispal, this cosy café was once part of an 18th-century palace. It has a beautiful courtyard, which retains many of its period features, where you can lounge on rattan armchairs and listen to classical music. Very select and elegant, it offers regular evening events and concerts in one of three different salons, each decorated in contrasting styles.

El Arenal

Coliseo

C. Almirante Lobo, 17
☎ 954 218 430
✆ 954 529 211
Open every day 8am-1am.

Coliseo

Located by the Puerta de Jerez, this is a cafeteria, restaurant, ice cream parlour and bakery all in one. Tapas are available at any time of day in its huge tiled, wooden bar and you can relax outside with a bowl of gazpacho or a dish of ice cream. Croissants are baked daily at around 5pm – just the time to find yourself at the bar or sitting at a table on the terrace.

Barrio de la Macarena

orno Macarena

. Resolana, 23
☎ 954 902 822
pen every day 8am-9pm.

f you're exhausted from hasing bargains at the stalls in he Alameda de Hércules and ootsore from exploring the Macarena district, you can stop ff here on your way to the asílica. This specialist bakery-um-delicatessen offers a fine rray of patisserie, preserves hade from Seville oranges and mpting ice creams.

Triana

orno San uenaventura

. Pagès del Corro, 55
☎ 954 331 926
☎ 954 337 998

n the other side of the river, this aroom has a selection of

pastries, sandwiches and buffet dishes that are quite enough to keep the wolf from the door.

San Lorenzo

Emperador Trajano

C. Trajano, 10
☎ 954 905 111
Open every day 8am-1am.

This café, with its exposed stonework, is hardly ever closed. Whether you're on your own or in company, you can have a snack on the hoof at the bar, or sit down to take your time over a leisurely lunch. The selection of patisserie and cakes are a wonderful treat at teatime – accompanied by one of their first-rate *café solo*.

Bar del Mar & PMN

C. Jesús del Gran Poder, 83

Located in the ultra-cool San Lorenzo district, this is certainly

one of the city's most stylish cafés, with a trendy Art Deco look. The atmosphere is relaxing and refined and from Thursday to Sunday you can listen to some great music here, while enjoying a selection of fresh, homemade cakes, all washed down with a wide range of coffees and teas.

Outside the city walls

Heladeria Milan

C. Arroyo, 53
☎ 954 537 843

This ice cream parlour specialises in handmade frozen yoghurt, with over 40 different flavours to choose from. You can add meringues and whipped cream or top them with maple syrup. All the products are made from completely natural ingredients and are totally delicious.

Shopping Practicalities

There's nothing like warm weather for shopping and in the early evening, after their siesta, the locals head off, alone or *en famille*, for a *paseo* (stroll) down Calle Sierpes and the surrounding area. You can meander down the pedestrianised streets, calling in at the bars, boutiques and shopping centres or simply window-shopping at both the trendy and more traditional stores, where you can get every conceivable kind of local product.

WHERE TO SHOP

Seville's busiest commercial area is in the city centre triangle formed by Plaza de San Francisco, Plaza del Salvador and Calle La Campana. The best-known shopping streets are Sierpes and Tetuán, where you can find modern outlets cheek by jowl with traditional shops selling typical local items such as *mantillas* (veils), *mantones* (shawls) and fans. The Barrio de Santa Cruz has a good selection of souvenir shops for tourists and there are a number of antique shops and smaller art galleries located around the Plaza del Alfalfa and near the Calle del Rey Don Pedro. If you've got your heart set on some of Seville's famous ceramics, then head for Triana.

OPENING HOURS

In general, shops are open Monday to Friday, from 10am to 2pm and from 5pm to 8pm, and on Saturday from 10am to 2pm only. These times are just a guide and they may vary by 30 minutes or so. If you want to make sure you don't miss the shops, the best times to go are between 10am and 1.30pm and 5.30pm and 8pm. In Sierpes, you can find some stores, such as Zara and Massimo Dutti, which stay open through the middle of the day. The bigger superstores tend to stay open from 10am to 9pm, Monday to Saturday.

FINDING YOUR WAY AROUND

Next to each address in the Shopping and Nightlife sections we have given a map reference to help you find its location on the map on pp. 138–139.

D

E

1

Calle Diego Martínez Barr

de Eduardo Dato

Enramadilla

venida

de la Buhaira

Avenida

Calle Ramón Carande

Calle C. Dr P. de Castro

Mor. Galván

C. Juan de Mata Carriazo

Avenida de la

C. Cap. Vigueras

Av. de Carlos V

Menéndez Pelayo

Borbolla

PZA DE ESPAÑA

Museo Arqueológico

2

Jardines del Alcázar

Av. Isabel la Católica

Parque de María Luisa

Av. del Cid

Av. de María Luisa

PZA DEL TRIUNFO

Reales Alcázar

C. San Fernando

La Universidad

ralda

Delicias

PUENTE DEL GENERALISIMO

PUERTA DE JEREZ

iral

de la Constitución

Av. de Roma

de las

Colón

Cristóbal

AV. PUENTE DE SAN TELMO

Calle Juan Sebastián

Calle Elcano

3

Torre del Oro

PZA DE CUBA

Calle

Calle de la Virgen de Luján

Asunción

estranza

Avenida de la República Argentina

Carranza

seo

de

Corro

del

Turia

Iglesia de Santa Ana

Pagés

del

Ramón y

UENTE ABEL II

) Calle

Iglesia de San Jacinto

Calle

Trabajo

Parque de los Príncipes

Feria de Abril

4

Calle

de

San Jacinto

Evangelista

Calle López de Gomara

de

Avenida

N

Triana

Av. de Coria

Av. de Alvar Núñez

Calle de R. Darío

de

0   200   400 m

0   200   400 yds

D

E

This guide was written by **Mercedes Escudero** and **Sophie Paumard**, with assistance from **Élodie Louvet**, **Jean-Pierre Marenghi** and **Magali Vidal**

Cover: **Thibault Reumaux**

Design: **Chrystel Arnould**

UK edition translated and edited by **Andrew Morton** and **Sheila Murphy**

Additional research and assistance: **Christine Bell**

We have done our best to ensure the accuracy of the information contained in this guide. However, addresses, phone numbers, opening times etc. inevitably do change from time to time, so if you find a discrepancy please do let us know. You can contact us at: HachetteTravel@philips-maps.co.uk or write to us at the address below.

Hachette Travel Guides provide independent advice. The authors and compilers do not accept any remuneration for the inclusion of any addresses in these guides.

Please note that we cannot accept any responsibility for any loss, injury or inconvenience sustained by anyone as a result of any information or advice contained in this guide.

Photo acknowledgements

Inside pages:
All the photographs in this guide were taken by **Laurent Parrault**, with the exception of those on the following pages:
Jacques Debru: p. 28 (t.l.)
Deauville Tourist Office: p. 11 (t., b.), 21 (t.l.)
Photothèque Hachette: p. 12 (b.l.), 15 (t.l.), 18 (b.r.), 20 (b.c.), 30 (c.l.), 31 (t.l., c.c., c.r.)

Cover:
Laurent Parrault, with the exception of the figures © Image Bank, Crowther and Carter (t.c.); © Image Bank, Werner Bokelberg (b.c.); © Photodisc, Ryan McVay (b.r.)

Back cover:
Laurent Parrault

Illustrations

Virginia Pulm

Distributed in the United States of America by Sterling Publishing Co., Inc.
387 Park Avenue South, New York, NY 10016-8810

A CIP catalogue for this book is available from the British Library

ISBN 0 54008 275 9

Hachette Travel Guides, c/o Philip's, 2–4 Heron Quays, London E14 4JP

Printed and bound in Slovenia.

HACHETTE TRAVEL GUIDES

A GREAT WEEKEND IN ...

Amsterdam	1 84202 145 1
Barcelona	0 54008 323 2
Berlin	1 84202 061 7
Brussels	1 84202 017 X
Budapest	0 54008 274 0
Dublin	1 84202 096 X
Florence	0 54008 322 4
Lisbon	1 84202 011 0
London	1 84202 168 0
Madrid	1 84202 095 1
Naples	1 84202 016 1
New York	0 54008 321 6
Paris	1 84202 001 3
Prague	1 84202 000 5
Rome	1 84202 169 9
Seville	0 54008 275 9
Venice	1 84202 018 8
Stockholm	0 54008 318 6
Vienna	1 84202 026 9

ROUTARD

Indulge your taste for travel with the ultimate food, drink and accommodation guides for the independent traveller.

Andalucia & Southern Spain	1 84202 028 5
Athens & the Greek Islands	1 84202 023 4
Belgium	1 84202 022 6
North Brittany	1 84202 020 X
California, Nevada & Arizona	1 84202 025 0
Canada	1 84202 031 5
Cuba	1 84202 062 5
Ireland	1 84202 024 2
Paris	1 84202 027 7
Provence & the Côte d'Azur	1 84202 019 6
Rome & Southern Italy	1 84202 021 8
Thailand	1 84202 029 3

VACANCES

Colourful, information-packed, leisure and activity guides. Hundreds of suggestions for things to do and sights to see.

Alsace	1 84202 167 2
The Ardèche	1 84202 161 3
The Basque Country	1 84202 159 1
Brittany	1 84202 007 2
Catalonia	1 84202 099 4
Corsica	1 84202 100 1
The Dordogne & Périgord	1 84202 098 6
French Alps	1 84202 166 4
Languedoc-Roussillon	1 84202 008 0
Normandy	1 84202 097 8
Poitou-Charentes	1 84202 009 9
Provence & the Côte d'Azur	1 84202 006 4
Pyrenees & Gascony	1 84202 015 3
South West France	1 84202 014 5